Copyright © 2023 Shie Rozow

All Rights Reserved. No part of this book may be used or reproduced in any manner whatsoever without written permission, except in the case of brief quotations in critical articles and reviews.

   First published in 2023
   ISBN 9798387370267

The information provided in this book does not, and is not intended to constitute legal advice; instead, all information, content, and materials available in this book are for general information purposes only. Readers of this book should contact their attorney to obtain advice with respect to any particular legal matter. No reader of this book should act or refrain from acting. the basis of information in this book without first seeking legal advice from counsel in the relevant jurisdiction.

Special thanks to
Jonathan Beard, Ashley Jarmack, Gayle Levant, Whitney Martin, Baraka May, Ben Newhouse, Alyssa Park, Ethan, Sheri and Zach Rozow, Dan and Abby Savell, Chris Tedesco, Robert Thies, and Gina Zimmitti.

Table of Contents

Introduction	1
Part One: Organization	3
Part Two: Budget	7
Part Three: Scheduling	17
Part Four: Recording Order	31
Part Five: Stem Considerations	49
Part Six: Pro Tools Session Prep	65
Part Seven: Remote Recording	83
Part Eight: File Naming Conventions	87
Addendum One: Score Mix	91
Addendum Two: Dub Session Prep	97
Final Thoughts	101

A Guide for Media Composers and Their Teams

Introduction

Scoring a feature film, documentary, TV show or video game is a major undertaking. Depending on where you are in your career and the budget of your project, you may be working with a team or doing it all by yourself. In this guide I will share all the factors and steps I believe should be considered and followed when preparing to record live musicians for your score. Whether you're going to spend 3 weeks recording a large symphonic orchestra, or a just record a single session with a soloist, the principles are the same.

I will cover technical considerations, creative considerations, and budget considerations covering everything from organization, to scheduling, to session prep, to file management, to delivering your mixed score to the client. I'm sure there are variations on how things are done among different people and teams, this is my attempt to share what I have learned over my 25 years in the industry. If you disagree with anything or have a different preferred

Preparing for Scoring Sessions

method that works well for you, by all means use it, this is how I like to do things to keep the process efficient. Following these steps has proven successful for me.

I hope this guide provides you with all the information you need to plan, budget, prepare and deliver your score efficiently and professionally.

A Guide for Media Composers and Their Teams

Part One
Organization

Keeping organized is key to a successful outcome. Organization begins by having a clear system to track your progress. This means having a clear list of every single cue that needs to be composed, start and end timecodes, durations, and the status of each cue so you know exactly where things are in the process and exactly what remains to be done and by when. There are various approaches to doing this. Some people like to use Cue Chronicle, others like CueDB.com or spottingnotes.com, yet others use bespoke database systems or Google Sheets. There is no right or wrong answer, as long as the solution you choose works well for you and your team.

A few years ago, I created a Google sheet to help me keep my own projects organized. I decided to freely share it with anyone

Preparing for Scoring Sessions

who might want to use it, and occasionally I update it, fixing bugs or adding new features. You can find my SR Show Cue Manager Google sheet on my website at www.shierozow.com in the blog section of my site, which you are free to use.

When recording live instruments, what truly matters isn't how long a cue is, but rather how much music you'll need to record for each cue. For example, if a 4-minute cue has a mixture of synths and live strings, what matters when planning for the recording session is how long the strings play within the cue. If they only play for 1 minute, then for recording purposes count this cue as 1 minute, not 4. However keep in mind that what you're really counting is the duration of chunks you'll record in a single take. If there are just a couple of bars of rest within a section, count them in your minute count. Generally, if there is less that 15 seconds of rests between chunks of music, I'll count those as a single chunk when measuring the duration, including those 15 seconds of rest. If there are more than 15 seconds of rests, I'll expect we'll stop at the end of the first chunk then start up again later, so I won't count those rests as part of my duration. If you're going to record different sections separately, do this for each section, so your total minute count for strings will likely be different than for winds or for brass, and so on.

It's not uncommon for orchestrators to split cues with lots of divisi into a couple of passes when recording. This is especially common when recording string sections on their own. Sometimes it's to make sure there are enough players on each note to achieve the desired sound. Sometimes it's separating short and long notes. The size of the section you have will influence how many passes you'll want to record. In instances where you plan to have multiple passes, make sure you add up the durations of all those passes when counting how many minutes you'll need to record. If you're working under a union contract, make sure you're not running afoul of union rules. Different unions have different rules, as do different recording locations even if they are not unionized.

For example, AFM musicians charge double to overdub within a single 3-hour session, making it very expensive. But there are cost-effective ways to handle multiple or overdub passes with LA AFM musicians. Option 1, if the passes are to separate long notes from short, or high from low, and you have a large enough section, you can simply ask some players not to play during the first pass, and then have the players who sat out play the second pass. This will not trigger overdub fees. If you have more than a single session, you can schedule the first pass in the morning session, and the second pass in the afternoon session. Being separate sessions, this is not considered overdubbing. Whatever the case, make sure you add up the duration of each pass when figuring out how many minutes you need to record. If you have 2 passes on a cue with 1 minute of strings, count that cue as 2 minutes to record, not 1. And always make sure you know the rules that govern your recording sessions and plan accordingly.

It's important to meet you client's expectations when planning sessions. On indie/low budget films, splits are usually minimal. But on higher budget films, or in some instances even on lower budget films a director might want various levels of separation for the dub stage, or you might want them in order to have better control when mixing your score. It's best to have these discussions early

Preparing for Scoring Sessions

so you can plan accordingly and avoid any unexpected surprises or conflicts.

Sometimes due to budget restrictions you can't afford to record everything and need to keep samples for some instruments. Sometimes it's more about the performance, you might absolutely love the sound of your samples and how they are programmed and don't wish to replace them with the real thing. Or you may just want to sweeten them rather than completely replace them. Depending on the style of music and personal preference, you may place different values on which instruments you want to record live, vs. which ones can stay "in-the-box." That said, in my experience the most common instruments that can stay samples and still sound very good are percussion instruments, piano, celeste, and mallets. This isn't to say those are the only options, just the ones I've most commonly seen during my career.

A Guide for Media Composers and Their Teams

Part Two
Budgeting

There are lots of factors that will affect the cost of producing your score. These include but are not limited to:

- How many splits you require.
- How many minutes you need to record.
- The size of your ensemble(s).
- Are there any soloists that need to be recorded?
- Music complexity.
- Where you record.
- Travel costs.
- Recording engineer costs.
- Mix costs.

Note: I did not include music editing because music editorial costs should be paid by the producers as part of their editorial budget and should not be part of your music budget. That's not

Preparing for Scoring Sessions

always the case, but always try to exclude music editorial costs from your deal, especially if you're on a package deal.

Splits

This may be obvious but consider that recording an orchestra in sections - for example recording strings, winds, and brass separately - will take longer than recording the entire orchestra performing together. Recording this way means more sessions, which means more days in the studio, which means higher studio costs. This will also increase your recording engineer costs as they are typically paid by the day and recording in sections means more days of recording.

Minutes

Again, this is obvious, but the more minutes you must record, the longer it'll take to record, meaning more studio time and all the costs associated with that. How many minutes you need to record will also affect your orchestration and music prep costs along with your mixing costs. Keep in mind that what matters when budgeting the recording sessions is how many minutes you're actually recording, which may not always match the duration of your cues. Again, if a cue is mostly electronic with only a little bit of live recording, the duration that matters is how much live material there is to record. Conversely if you need to record a cue in 2 or 3 passes, the number of minutes you need to record will be higher than the duration of the cue, taking longer to record. When planning how much time you'll need for your mix, what maters is the actual duration of the cues regardless of how much is live vs. samples.

Ensemble

Another obvious consideration is your ensemble size. The more musicians you have in your ensemble, the higher the costs. Paying 4 musicians to record a string quartet will cost a fraction of paying 40 musicians to record a string section. Choir costs can be very different than those of a soloist or instrumentalist. You can hire a handful of musicians directly but hiring a large group or orchestra will likely require a contractor, meaning contracting costs. In addition, the ensemble size will affect your orchestration costs. Orchestrators typically charge per page, and how much they charge per page changes depending on how many staves are on each page. This will also affect your music prep costs, as preparing and printing lots of parts will understandably be more expensive than preparing and printing fewer parts. Naturally, if you have the time and opt to do your own orchestrations and prep, you'll save money, but in such cases don't underestimate your own printing costs such as ink/toner and paper, which will vary based on how many parts you print.

Soloists

If your score requires soloists, expect to pay a premium for their performances compared to section players. Also consider how and where you record them, for example soloists recording themselves at their home studio will likely cost less than having them record in a studio since you'll be saving on studio and engineer costs.

Music Complexity

The more complex and challenging your music, the longer it will take to record. To offer an example, when working on Stargirl with Pinar Toprak we recorded strings, and sometimes brass and even woodwinds for each episode. Big, complicated action cues might take half an hour to record a single cue, and then we might record 4 or 5 other simple cues adding up to more minutes than that single complicated cue in the remaining 20 minutes of the hour. The style of writing will determine how quickly you can record and therefore how much recording time you will need. This will also affect your mix as described later. As a rule of thumb, I tend to plan for an average of 5-6 minutes per hour when recording orchestra in LA, London or Glasgow, 4-5 minutes when recording remotely in Europe. I expect just 3-3.5 minutes per hour when working with choir, and just 2.5-3 minutes per hour when working with solo vocalists. If the music is particularly challenging, I may plan on less minutes per hour, if it's relatively simple I'll plan for the upper end of the range.

Location

Where you record will have a major effect on your costs. Scoring in LA under an AFM contract will likely cost more than recording locally as a dark date. The studio costs of recording at the Barbara Streisand Scoring Stage at Sony are different than those of recording at Silent Zoo in Glendale. Scoring in London or Scotland will be more expensive than scoring in Nashville or Budapest. Each location has different cost structures, too. Some locations offer their scoring stage for free like when recording with the Royal Scottish National Orchestra (RSNO) in Glasgow, while others charge a daily fee, while others pro-rate for single sessions and others charge an hourly rate. Some locations cover the costs of printing parts, most don't. As indicated above, where you record can affect how many minutes you can comfortably record per hour, affecting how many hours you need to record your score. Another variable when recording overseas is the exchange rate. There are lots of variables to navigate depending on where you record. The same is true for mixing, more on that later.

Recording Engineer

Some locations include an in-house recording engineer along with their Pro Tools operator/recordist as part of their pricing. Others expect you to bring in your own engineer or can recommend or even provide an engineer at an additional cost. As with anyone in the freelance world, different engineers charge different rates. Most charge by the day, so the more days of recording you need, the more your recording engineer will cost. As mentioned above, if you're bringing an engineer to a remote studio, there are travel costs, but sometimes there maybe travel costs even if you're not. For example, when recording remotely in Glasgow with the RSNO you could hire a local engineer, or you might want to bring in an engineer from London, in which case you need to account not just for their fees, but also their travel costs from England to Glasgow.

Orchestration

When recording live musicians, especially an ensemble or orchestra, your music needs to be orchestrated. Even if recording

Preparing for Scoring Sessions

remotely, you will likely use a local orchestrator or orchestration team, though not necessarily and costs can vary greatly. If you're recording in LA under AFM contract, expect to pay at minimum union rates, which are based on how many pages there are to orchestrate (a page is defined as 4 bars), and how many staves per page. Keep in mind that many orchestrators often charge above scale. If this is a non-union gig, prices can vary greatly and range from a per page rate, to a per minute rate. Here are some approximate sample orchestration cost estimates for comparison based on orchestrating 60 minutes of orchestral music, which is typically 400-500 score pages.

	AFM rates	Non-Union Low Budget	Non-Union Mid Budget	Non-Union Big Budget
Page rate	$35-80 per page	$25 per page	$100 per page	$120-160 per page
Minute rate	N/A	$190 per minute	$750 per minute	$1,200 per minute
Orchestration Cost	$14,000 - $40,000	$10,000 - $12,500	$40,000 - $50,000	$48,000 - $80,000

Music prep

Once orchestration is complete, parts will need to be prepared, and printed. No matter where you record, you'll need to have someone print the scores and all the parts, tape them and deliver to the stage. If recording overseas, you'll send PDFs to the vendor you use, and they'll handle the printing there. Some include this cost within their fees, others will specify the printing costs as their own line item. Using the example above of about 60 minutes of music for a 50-piece orchestra, you can expect prep costs to be around $14,000.

Mix Costs

While not strictly part of the session prep and session costs, mixing costs should be accounted for when preparing your budget. I have an entire section on that later (see Addendum 1). However here are some basics. Many of the factors mentioned above will affect your mix costs. Different engineers have different fees, as do their assistants (if they use an assistant). Mixing studio costs also vary depending on where the mix takes place. Using the penthouse at Abbey Road Studios will incur a different fee than mixing at The Mix Lab in Santa Monica or Technicolor Sound on the Paramount Studios lot to name a few examples. How many minutes need to be mixed will affect how many days your mixing engineer needs to get the job done. Reminder, you need to count the total duration of all cues, not just the total duration of live recordings as described in the previous section when calculating how much there is to mix. How complex the music is will also affect how long it takes to deliver a great mix. For example, mixing a full orchestra with 200 tracks of pre-records will take a lot longer than mixing a small ensemble with no pre-records.

Score Coordinators

When working on medium and big budget productions, it's not unusual to have a score-coordinator involved. This person will help handle the budget, scheduling and coordinating with all the different parties involved. If you use a freelance score coordinator expect to pay them for their services. In my experience, more often than not they're invaluable and worth every penny.

Travel

If you record at a distant location from where you live, you may incur travel costs. Remote recording is always a possibility, but if you choose to travel there in person, make sure you account for travel costs like flights, train rides, taxis/ride-share/car rental, and lodging. If you're bringing an assistant with you, or a recording engineer or orchestrator or conductor, or maybe a spouse or family members with you, include their travel costs, too. Keep in mind that if you're flying to Europe or other distant locations with a significant time-zone difference, you'll likely want to arrive 2 or 3 days before the first day of recording to allow yourself some time to adjust to the new time-zone. Conversely, if you're flying from LA to Nashville, which is a relatively short flight and only a 2-hour time-difference, arriving the night before might be fine. You should also account for a per-diem for engineers, orchestrators, or a conductor if you choose to bring those with you to a remote recording location. Keep these considerations in mind when budgeting your travel costs.

Other

There are other factors to consider that may come up depending on your situation and needs. For example, if you want to hire a film crew to shoot behind the scenes footage, consider those costs, along with the costs of editing said footage. Depending on where and how and you're paying your musicians there may be payroll or administrative fees to consider. There may be equipment rental costs involved. There may be cartage costs, this is typical for percussion, and large instruments like basses or harps among others. If you're recording a piano, you should account for piano tuning costs. Some locations offer buyout fees if you wish not to incur any back-end residual payments. If working oversees, exchange rates can affect your costs, this can be significant especially on larger projects. These are all additional things you should keep in mind when creating your budget.

Resources

I created a Google sheet to help me build budgets, which again I decided to freely share it with anyone who might want to use it, and update it occasionally, fixing bugs or adding new features. You can find my **SR Budget Estimate Template** on my website at www.shierozow.com in the blog section of my site, which you are also free to use.

Below is a budget breakdown comparison for recording 60 minutes with 50 strings in different locations to give you some idea of cost differences and considerations. This budget assumes recording at an average pace of 5 minutes per hour, meaning 12 hours of recording over 2 days with 2 x 3-hour sessions per day. EU and UK prices converted to US dollars using exchange rates as of 12/13/22. Actual prices may vary based on current exchange rates. Also, these are my best estimates extrapolated from various real budgets of projects I worked on in 2022.

For exact numbers please consult a contractor as these may not be 100% accurate, but they should give you a good ballpark idea of the cost differences at various locations.

Preparing for Scoring Sessions

Sample Budget Comparison

	Budapest	Bulgaria	Glasgow	Nashville	London	LA Non-AFM	LA AFM
Musicians	$19,995	$14,067	$51,992	$62,400	$51,992	$78,000	$72,634
Cartage	Included	Included	Included	$1,176	$1,300	$700	$1,020
CM/Leaders	Included	$3,037	$1,040	Included	$1,040	Included	Included
Conductor	Included	$702	$3,321	$2,400	$3,321	$3,000	$3,112
Buyout Fee	N/A	N/A	$8,481	N/A	$8,481	N/A	N/A
Scoring Stage	Included	$893	Free	$5,000	$12,300	$12,000	$12,000
Recording Engineer	Included	Included w/ studio	$3,690	$2,400	$3,690	$4,000	$4,000
Pro Tools Operator	Included	Included w/ studio	$1,000	$1,100	$1,000	$2,000	$2,000
Stage Manager	N/A	N/A	$1,040	N/A	N/A	N/A	N/A
Session Producer	N/A	$702	N/A	N/A	N/A	N/A	N/A
Setup	Included	$74	Included	Included w/ studio	Included w/ studio	$1,200	$1,200
Librarian/Printing	Included	$638	$5,000	$5,000	$5,000	$5,000	$5,000
Contractor	Included	$2,037	$8,758	$4,200	$8,758	$4,500	$4,600
Conductor Travel	N/A	N/A	$246	N/A	N/A	N/A	N/A
Conductor Hotel	N/A	N/A	$498	N/A	N/A	N/A	N/A
Admin/Payroll Fees	N/A	$255	N/A	$3,178	N/A	$3,935	$12,155
Contingency	$1,000	$1,150	$4,500	$4,500	$5,000	$5,000	$5,000
Total	$20,995	$23,555	$89,556	$91,354	$101,882	$119,335	$122,720

LA Non-AFM, it may be possible to get a sliding scale depending on the project type

AFM based on TV/Streaming Scale, costs can vary depending on the type of contract the project falls under. Musicians' costs include $60,773.10 in wages, $7,006.44 AFM Pension & $4,854.00 AFM Health & Welfare.

A Guide for Media Composers and Their Teams

Part Three
Scheduling

When scheduling, the first consideration is how much time is needed to record the score. As mentioned previously, the complexity of the music will determine how many minutes you can reasonably expect to record per hour. Where you choose to record can also affect this calculation. Los Angeles, London and Glasgow musicians are some of the best on the planet, Nashville musicians are also excellent and rival the best, but as you venture elsewhere, good as they are, the quality of the musicians, crews and facilities don't quite match up. This means you may need more time to record the same amount of music compared to recording in LA or London.

Another consideration is how you record your score. Will you be recording the entire orchestra at once, or individual sections?

Preparing for Scoring Sessions

Recording in sections will take longer than recording everyone at once, though some sections will have less minutes to record and go faster than others. For example, recording 60 minutes when splitting up strings, brass, and woodwinds won't take 3 times as long as recording those 60 minutes with the entire orchestra together, but it will take significantly longer.

In terms of minutes recorded per hour, here are some minute counts based on my experience over the years. I touched on this above and I've gone faster and slower depending on the nature of the music, the composer and where we were recording, but here are some guidelines to give you some idea of what to reasonably expect.

In my experience, recording a full orchestra performing together takes longer than recording individual sections in terms of how many minutes one can record per hour. In my experience about 3-4 minutes per hour on average, 5 minutes if the music isn't too challenging and the sessions are well organized. Recording strings only, or strings and woodwinds, which can often work well together can achieve at least 4-5 minutes per hour. Winds on their own can often achieve 5-6 minutes an hour comfortably. Brass can usually manage about 5-6.5 minutes an hour. Percussion tends to manage 5-7 minutes per hour when recording all percussion instruments together (meaning several percussionists playing different instruments at the same time). If you're splitting out timpani or other instruments, half that minute per hour estimate or double the amount of time you allot them, however you prefer to think of it will achieve the same result. Recording harp, piano and/or celeste on their own tends to go pretty quickly, 5-7 minutes per hour. Choir and solo vocals seem to take the longest. I try to schedule a rate of 3-3.5 minutes per hour for choir, 4 if the music is easy and I'm feeling ambitious. For soloists I aim for 2.5 - 3.5 minutes per hour depending on the singer and the music. Again, these are just ballpark numbers based on my own experiences working with a variety of composers and teams with orchestras all over the world, your own experience may differ.

Recording Rules

I touched on this above briefly. Different locations have different standard rules, or guidelines to how they conduct their sessions. When recording in Los Angeles under AFM contract most often you'll be working in 3-hour sessions. Going beyond 3 hours constitutes overtime, which accrues in 15-minute increments. Musicians expect 10-minute breaks at the end of every hour, so in a 3-hour session there are actually 2.5 hours of playing time. If you think you may need OT, it's best to alert your contractor, who will alert the musicians ahead of time, but they are generally prepared to stay up to an hour of OT if necessary.

In the UK we can book either 3 or 4-hour sessions. 3-hour sessions include a single 15-minute break halfway through the session, usually after 90 minutes, leaving another 75 minutes of recording after the break for a total of 2:45 of recording time. 4-hour sessions include a single 20-minute break halfway through for 3:40 of total recording time. Unlike the US, staying for unplanned overtime is entirely voluntary in the UK. I've only ever gone into OT in the UK once and it was just 15 minutes, so we had no issues, but it's important to realize that if you have significant overages, you

Preparing for Scoring Sessions

could lose some of your musicians. If you think you might need more time, it's better to plan a 4-hour session rather than a 3-hour session in advance. The rules in most other European locations are similar to those in the UK though some locations allow for 2-hour sessions, too. Break schedules also tend to be a single break halfway through the session. Finally, UK union rules allow for a maximum of 8 minutes of recorded music per hour. As long as you don't record more than 24 minutes in a 3-hour session or 32 minutes in a 4-hour session, they will not have any issues if you record at a pace that's faster than 8 minutes per hour in any single hour. I once recorded about 10 minutes of percussion in one hour because the music was easy, but we then only recorded about 5-6 minuts per hour for the remaining two hours so our total was less that 24 minutes, which is what they enforce.

As described earlier, in the US under AFM rules, doing overdubs is very expensive. In other places it doesn't incur any additional costs at all, it just takes more time to record. Make sure you find out what the rules and the process will be wherever you record so you can calculate how many hours you'll need and plan accordingly.

Furthermore, since the COVID-19 pandemic, rules have changed and differ significantly from one location to another. These restrictions include testing requirements, which can affect your budget, masking, how many people can play together, longer breaks, whether triple sessions are allowed or not, and so on. In some places there are no restrictions at all anymore. Make sure to find out what COVID-19 restrictions (if any) affect you when planning your recording schedule.

Session order

OK, you've figured out how many sessions you need, now it's time to schedule them. But how do you figure out what to record first? As is often the case, the style of the music should dictate the ideal session order, but sometimes there are other practical considerations that'll supersede the ideal scenario, like player availability, or studio setup time.

When recording orchestral scores in sections, I prefer to start with the string section, followed by woodwind section, followed by brass. It's not uncommon to record strings and woodwinds together. It's also common to record harp(s) with the string section, either in the room with the strings or in a booth. If you're recording live percussion, piano or celesta, those would typically come next. Musically speaking, the specific order isn't critical, so practical considerations such as musician availability or studio setup time can determine the schedule. However, if a score features a piano or some other instrument heavily, you may want to record it either with the strings if feasible, or before recording the strings so they have that reference for their performance. Finally, if recording choir, that'll be the last thing I record whenever possible, so they can tune to the orchestra. However, I have had situations where the choir was pre-recorded to the mockups before we recorded the orchestra, always due to practical considerations rather than musical ones.

If there are occasional string, woodwind, or brass solos, I'll record them during the corresponding sessions. However, if there are extensive solos, or other unusual instruments soloing, like world-winds, guitar, lute, cimbalom, accordion, solo vocals or whatever

Preparing for Scoring Sessions

else it may be, it's often best to pre-record those before recording the orchestra. This can be done in-studio or remotely depending on your circumstances. Sometimes I'll record some instruments in advance, and others, where the orchestral performance will more meaningfully affect the soloist's performance later.

Setup time

Keep in mind that recording will always require setup time. Whether you're recording a full orchestra, a section or a soloist recording him/herself from home, there will be some setup time involved. Sessions need to be prepared for recording, if you're recording on a stage or in a studio, seats must be arranged on the floor, microphones must be placed. If recording piano, celeste, percussion or some other instruments, the instruments themselves need to be brought in and set up. Setting up to record 50 strings is more labor intensive and time consuming than setting up for just 8 woodwinds. Setting up a piano requires tuning before the session and setting up percussion requires bringing in crates of instruments and preparing each player's station, so setup times can vary depending on what you're recording. Make sure to account for setup time when planning your recording schedule. It's best to have a conversation with the studio staff to find out how much time they need to change the room from one setup to another. When working in large spaces it's often possible to setup for the entire orchestra at once, so there is no setup time required between sessions recording different sections.

Sometimes you need a setup day, which is quite common when preparing to record a big score with an orchestra. Other times you need an extra hour or two of break time between sessions to allow enough time for the staff to change the room from one setup to the next. And sometimes a late start gives the studio staff enough time for an early morning setup instead. It's important to discuss setup requirements with the studio staff and your recording engineer when planning you session schedule to make sure your plan is realistic. I've had to re-arrange the scheduling of sessions to accommodate setup requirements to keep things as efficient as possible.

I recently worked on a project where for a variety of reasons we couldn't record exactly as we'd ideally have scheduled things if musicality were the only consideration. Instead, in order to get everything done within the allotted time we recorded strings and harp for 2.5 days, then did 2 percussion sessions on the afternoon/evening of the 3rd day. Day 4 consisted of 2x3-hour sessions with woodwinds. Day 5 consisted of another 3-hour session with woodwinds in the morning, followed by a 3-hour break to give the studio staff time to both have lunch and change the room for a 4-hour celesta session. On day 6 we did just a 4-hour session of brass, which was all we needed, and left the studio staff plenty of time to change the room for a 40-voice choir, which we recorded the next morning followed by a 3-hour break before doing our final session, which was a 3-hour piano session. We also pre-recorded a handful of soloists before recording the orchestra, all of those were done remotely.

I worked on a different project where we needed to record strings and woodwinds together in Budapest, traditional choir also in Budapest, and Balkan choir in Bulgaria. Ideally, we would

Preparing for Scoring Sessions

have recorded the strings and winds first, but due to availability, we did the Balkan choir before recording the strings and woods. As you can see, there's what's ideal, and then there's what's possible. The trick is to make sure you find the balance between the two to achieve the most cost-effective and efficient schedule possible.

Time of Day

In addition to scheduling based on all the above considerations, think about what time of the day the session(s) will take place. As you can see in the example I gave above, when recording celesta and piano we made those afternoon/evening sessions. Not only was this to accommodate setup time, it's also less hassle to ask just one or two musicians to do an evening session vs. an entire orchestra or a full section. When doing remote-recordings in other time-zones consider the time difference. Sure, it's no fun to pull an all-nighter, or wake up super-early, but it might be necessary depending on the location. Many European locations offer late starts (local time) to make it easier for us in Los Angeles. But if you're scheduling 7, 8 or even 9 hours of recording, they'll need to start earlier local time so they're not in the studio late into the night, meaning less convenient hours for us in Los Angeles. In some places the cost is the same, or the difference is minimal if recording is done in one day or two. It might be better to do 8 hours over 2 days with a 3-hour session followed by a 2-hour session on day 1 and another 3-hour session on day 2 than trying to do 2 4-hour sessions back-to-back. This will mean they can start later local time, meaning a less inconvenient time for you in Los Angeles, and they won't stay late, meaning they're less likely to get tired, which could affect their performances.

Contingencies

It's always good to have a plan B in case things don't go as expected. For example, above I described having 3-hour breaks between sessions to allow time for the studio staff to have lunch and setup for the next session. They didn't need 3 hours, 2 would have sufficed, the extra hour allowed us to go into overtime during the previous session if necessary. It was part of our contingency plan. Generally, I prefer to avoid triple sessions in a single day for several reasons. First, it makes for long days and it's difficult to stay focused for that long. Next, evening sessions often mean players have already played 6 hours earlier in the day so they'll be tired, which may affect their performances. Finally, it leaves no wiggle room for contingencies like adding a bit of overtime if needed. Note that due to COVID restrictions most locations no longer allow triple sessions, and some European locations never allowed them at all. When it comes to choir, it's best not to go beyond 2x3-hour sessions in a day. I've even planned sessions where we only did a single 3-hour afternoon or early evening session following an instrumental morning session 2 days in a row, so the singers never go beyond 3 hours at a time.

Booking Sessions

When planning to record, it's best to reach out to the studios where you wish to record as soon as possible to inquire about studio availability and putting holds on dates that work for you (assuming they're available). A hold means you've informed the studio that you intend to record on said dates so if another client wants to use those same dates, the studio will give you the opportunity to

Preparing for Scoring Sessions

either confirm your dates or release them to the other client. If your preferred dates aren't available and you can schedule different dates, that's great, but you may want to put a 2nd or even 3rd hold on your ideal dates. 2nd and 3rd holds mean you're next in line for those dates should the 1st hold release them and they become available. As the name 2nd and 3rd hold implies if a 1st hold releases, the 2nd hold becomes the presumptive new 1st hold, and the 3rd becomes the presumptive 2nd hold. Whomever has the 3rd hold will only be notified if whomever has the 2nd hold also released the dates. Similarly, if alternative dates don't work and you decide to go elsewhere, it doesn't hurt to put a 2nd or even 3rd hold at your preferred location just in case the dates become available at which point you could choose to release your holds at your 2nd choice location and record at your 1st choice location after all.

 Keep in mind that studios can book up well in advance, often months in advance, so it's good to get dates on hold as soon as possible. When booking early you may not know exactly how much studio time you need, or even exactly what type of ensemble you'll need. That's OK, a good idea is to book a little bit more time than your best early estimate. As you get further into the project, you'll get a better idea of your actual needs and can adjust accordingly, which often means releasing days you've learned you won't need. Keep in mind that if you release holds a the very last minute, you may still be required to pay for those dates, or pay a fee. When putting a hold on a studio, find out when you need to confirm or release dates without incurring any costs and plan accordingly. If working with a contractor, they can often handle this for you.

Session Delivery

As discussed above when considering setup time, the studio's recordist (or person doing a solo remote home-recording) will need time to prepare the recording sessions. In the case of studios, they'll expect that you deliver Pro Tools sessions into which they will add whatever tracks they need for the recording. However, some musicians use other DAWs for home recording, meaning they have to build their own sessions from scratch using audio & MIDI files you send them. Even if you're sending them immaculate Pro Tools sessions, which I'll teach you how to prepare below, the recordist will still need to create the empty tracks for the recording session, route all the outputs, and setup the recording console for the engineer, all of which takes time.

Therefore, it's important to discuss how and when you'll deliver your materials and to whom. Will you be bringing a hard drive with you to the stage? Will you be providing a dropbox or box link? Or perhaps you'll send an Aspera or Wetransfer or Hightail delivery? Consider how much time will be needed for uploading and downloading the materials and consider time-zones when working across the globe to make sure the files arrive with ample time for the recipient to receive them and do their prep work.

When working on major feature films, video security is heightened and it's not unusual to have the assistant picture editor create a specially watermarked set of video files for the stage. It's also common for those QT files to have different specs than the ones you prefer, and they may be sent to the stage directly from the editing room. Make sure you or someone on your team is coordinating this, so everyone is on the same page.

Preparing for Scoring Sessions

Session Departure

After the recording is done, you need to receive the recorded sessions along with all the recorded audio so you can prepare them to go on to the mix. Again, it's important to discuss how this is done in advance to have a game-plan in place. When planning your entire schedule, including mixing, consider how much time it will take to receive the sessions and prepare them for the next step and make sure you provide time in your schedule for this.

Mix Prep

The recording sessions are over, congrats. You've received all the sessions, now you need to prepare them for the mix. Once again, make sure you schedule enough time for this step. How much time you'll need depends on various factors. In some cases, you or a member of your team will want to go through everything to create the comps and clean up the sessions before they go to the mixer. In other cases, the mixer might have a brilliant assistant who will handle this task. In the former case you'll need more time in your schedule between receiving the materials and sending them to your mixer, in the latter you may be able to immediately forward those sessions directly to them which may not require any additional time in your schedule at all. At the risk of sounding like a broken record, make sure you have these discussions early so when you build your schedule you plan accordingly. I discuss mix prep in more detail further along this booklet.

Mix

An important part of scheduling is how many mix days are

needed. Once again, this is something you want to figure out and plan well in advance. If you don't know how much time your mixer will need, have a conversation with him or her to help you plan properly. As always, the style and complexity of the music will determine how quickly it can be mixed. Different mixers also mix at different rates. Budget and time limitations could force mixing within a certain amount of time even if it means mixing more minutes per day than is ideal. Keep in mind that in such cases the level of detail of the mix will be sacrificed. In my experience most mixers can comfortably handle 5-8 minutes a day when working on a typical orchestral film score, which usually includes choir and quite a few pre-records. Particularly complex scores, or cues will take longer, simpler material can be mixed faster. This average includes addressing mix notes. After all mixes are finished and approved, your mixer will need a day or so to print all the stems for the dub stage, make sure when scheduling you're keeping at least one day for printing on your calendar. In some cases, mixing can overlap with the dub, in which case, printing will happen periodically to make sure you receive the mixes you need when you need them, again if this is the case make sure you discuss this with your mixer in advance and have a plan in place.

As with the scoring stage (or individual soloists doing remote recording) it's important to discuss and plan for file delivery and departure to and from the mix so everyone involved knows what to expect and is prepared accordingly.

Preparing for Scoring Sessions

Part Four
Recording Order

Once you've got all your sessions planned, the order in which you record your cues can greatly affect how quickly and efficiently the session goes. In this section I'll discuss the factors I consider when deciding on the cue record order within each session to keep things moving as efficiently as possible.

First Cue Considerations

Picking your first cue can set the tone for the session. The musicians are fresh, but not yet warmed up. Their instruments aren't yet warmed up, which affects intonation. And your recording engineer is hearing the result of his or her setup for the first time, often leading to making some mic placement or other adjustments. With this in mind, I try to find a cue that's around

Preparing for Scoring Sessions

2 minutes long that ideally has a wide dynamic range and isn't particularly challenging. If no such cue exists, I'll opt for a louder cue. This allows the engineer to make sure no inputs are overloading, and all the levels are good. It lets the musicians warm up and get comfortable, easing into the session. The reason I look for a cue of this length is that it's not very long, which is good for warm-up purposes, but also long enough for the engineer to adjust his/her settings by the time you have a good take. If you choose a short cue, you may end up with a good take, but your engineer asking for one more because the settings weren't quite there, which wastes time.

Group Similar Cues Together

Often there are similar cues throughout a score, by which I mean cues that use the same theme, and/or have a similar vibe/feel to them. Grouping those together is a great way to keep things moving quickly and efficiently. The first cue of a particular vibe will usually take the longest because you're homing in on the sound you're after. Doing subsequent cues with a similar vibe right away means you can let the musicians know the next few cues have the same feel and the very first read will already be pretty close as whatever performance nuances the musicians applied before will automatically be applied again. I've had 1 take wonders using this method, though I always get a 2nd safety take just in case. When grouping cues, I like to program the longest of the cues first, followed by progressively shorter cues whenever possible. In my experience, this creates a sense of momentum and keeps things moving along better than keeping it random or going in the other direction.

Prioritize

Usually, musicians are fresher and more alert at the beginning of the day, and tire as the day progresses. The same is true for everyone on the crew for that matter. Therefore, I like to program challenging cues early in a session after the musicians have had a chance to warm up. Often that means doing big, demanding action cues before switching to dramatic, emotional, or lighthearted cues, that tend to be less challenging. As I mentioned above, I like to group similar cues together, but it's equally important to consider how challenging a cue is, especially if it's a long cue. If they're relatively short, it's probably fine to record 2 or 3 challenging cues back-to-back. However, consider how long you're keeping your players working on difficult music. You want to give them breaks following challenging cues to catch their breath (literally and figuratively). One way to do this is to program things so that difficult cues are followed by easy ones. This breaks the grouping, but it's OK, these are all considerations, not hard-and-fast rules, and it's important to prioritize what's most important. Giving musicians breathers after challenging sections is more important than staying in the same vibe.

Another approach is to program cues so that the session break (or breaks depending on where you're recording) takes place after challenging cues so the musicians literally get a break. You can then jump right into another challenging cue after the break. The only exception is when coming back after a lunch or dinner break since those are longer breaks. More on that below.

Sometimes there is more to record than is realistic, or it might be very challenging to get everything done in the allotted time. I've

Preparing for Scoring Sessions

seen this especially in episodic TV. In such cases I also prioritize cues by importance (regardless of difficulty level) and make sure I program important cues closer to the front or middle of sessions rather than towards the end, where we might not get to them. I also like to have a contingency plan for these scenarios, where if the budget permits I know I can go into some overtime if needed, but by getting all the must-record cues out of the way first, I'm less likely to use up OT for low priority cues. More on contingencies below.

If multiple sessions are planned, there's no need for a warmup cue at the beginning of the afternoon or evening session. The musicians and instruments are usually ready to go, but considering they've just had an hour-long break and some food, it's nice to ease in a bit rather than immediately jump in with something particularly difficult. Ideally, if possible, I try to knock out all the challenging cues in the morning session, but if it's not possible, then I aim to finish them early in the 2nd session. If there are multiple days of recording, I may leave additional challenging cues to the next morning instead of the afternoon.

Remember that challenging cues will take longer to record than easy ones. As you plan your order and minute count, you may expect fewer minutes to be recorded in the first hour or two than in later hours where you'll move faster recording easier cues.

Break Schedule

Make sure you know the break schedule of the location where you are recording when planning your recording order. As described earlier, the rules are different for different orchestras, and knowing how much actual recording time you have and when the breaks take place will allow you to plan accordingly. Planning for recording under AFM rules in LA will look different than planning to record in London, Bratislava, or Berlin to name a few possibilities.

Ensemble Size and Contingencies

Most projects include a variety of cues, some requiring larger ensembles, while others could work just as well with a smaller ensemble. Sometimes if there are multiple sessions, you can shed players from one session to the next, which can stretch your budget allowing you to achieve more with a limited budget. I once worked on a project with a $100,000 total recording budget for four sessions over two days. The plan was to record the entire orchestra together, but we couldn't afford that over the span of four sessions. After creating a detailed instrumentation breakdown of all the cues, I realized we didn't need a full wind or brass section for all cues, and some cues would work with a smaller string session, too. By reducing the size of the orchestra from one session to the next, I created 4 different ensembles and got the budget down from being nearly $20,000 over budget to just under our $100,000 limit, with a small contingency available, which we used for 15 minutes of overtime in our final session. That was a 20% saving by simply being well organized and surgical about planning for our specific needs. The music wasn't compromised in any way.

Using this same concept, consider your instrumentation when prioritizing cues. For example, if you're recording strings, and some cues only use violins and viole, but no celli or basses, it may be smart to save those for the end of your session. That way if you

Preparing for Scoring Sessions

need to go into OT you can let the viola, cello and bass players go, and you'll only incur OT costs for the players you keep. Same concept applies well with brass, often there are cues with horns only. Keep those for the end, and if you must go into overtime, you can let the rest of the brass choir go, minimizing your OT costs. Same goes for soloists. If you're planning to record any solos within a section session, program those at the end of your recording order for the same reason, keeping just 1 musician is obviously cheaper than keeping an entire section. Use these concepts to have contingencies in place in case you can't get everything you need done in the allotted time. I think it's worth reiterating that if you think you might need overtime it's important to have enough time between sessions to allow for OT in the first place, as discussed in the previous section.

Writing Tips

Your writing and how it is notated and copied can affect how quickly or slowly your musicians can record your music. Know your instruments and what's difficult or hard for different ones. Different instruments have different characteristics therefore what might be difficult on one isn't on another and vice versa. The same cue can be exceptionally difficult for one section, but easy for another. Key choices can make a huge difference, sometimes transposing your cue up or down a mere half step can impact how difficult it is to perform. How well your score and parts are prepared and look on the printed page will also affect your rate of progress. Here are some very rough guidelines of things to keep in mind when writing for different sections. Keep in mind these are very broad strokes, there are some great books on orchestrations that go into far more detail. A good orchestrator and copyists can help mitigate these issues, too.

General considerations

- Make sure your score and parts are properly laid out. Bad looking scores and parts are harder to sightread, which will slow things down.
- Watch your page turns, and make sure they are planned out well. If they aren't, or there isn't a good place for a page turn, you'll have to do pickups, which will slow things down.
- Make sure enharmonic spellings are correct. Wrong enharmonic spellings will slow things down.
- Make sure transposing parts are properly transposed.
- Include clear directions, articulations, phrase markings and dynamics.
- Most players don't like sightreading more than 3-4 ledger lines above or below the staff. If the music sits in that range for more than just a few notes, use 8va/8vb or switch to a different clef if appropriate. Flautists and violin players are the exception and are used to reading many ledger lines above the staff.
- If you're writing something challenging, reach out to your players early and have them look over tricky passages. Sometimes they can suggest slight changes that could make a big impact on playability, avoiding problems long before you get to the recording sessions.
- Rehearse tricky sections rather than simply repeating the entire cue over and over. Working through those pas-

Preparing for Scoring Sessions

sages rather than simply doing another take of the entire cue will lead to a subsequent take likely being successful.

Strings

- When writing fast passages that move up and down quickly, don't write more than one 5th interval in a row, unless it can be played as a harmonic.
- Large jumps, especially more than an octave can be tricky and often don't work very well.
- Artificial harmonics above 4th position on the violin E strings don't normally sound great.
- When writing non-divisi double stops, 3rds and 6ths are easiest. 4th and 5th are uncomfortable and can be difficult to tune. 2nds and 7th should be avoided unless they involve using open strings, in which case they can work.
- Consider your section size when writing divisi parts. A lot of divisi in a small section can affect the overall sound, making it sound more like a collection of soloists than a section.

Woodwinds

- Wind players don't like multiple parts on multiple staves, they prefer individual parts for each instrument. The only exception is if switching from one instrument to the next with ample to time to make the switch (i.e. switching from concert flute to alto flute and then back), in which case the instrument change will be indicated within a single staff.

- Flute in the low register is fairly soft compared to the rest of the instrument. Orchestrate accordingly if it's a part you'd like to he heard. Otherwise prepare to stripe it if there is a lot of other sounds/textures going on.
- The oboe is quite different than the flute, it's difficult to project in the higher register, and the low register tends to get honky. Writing high stuff for the oboe is harder to perform than on a flute. The oboe also doesn't blend like other woodwinds, use it appropriately, or you might find yourself asking it to tacet, or striping it.
- Playing quietly at the top of the register is hard for most woodwinds. For example, instead of ppp high on a flute, consider a piccolo. Instead of playing high quiet parts on bassoon consider using an English horn or bass oboe instead.
- The low register of a piccolo is a very pretty color, but it's difficult to project. If that's what you're after, you'll likely want to stripe it or have the player in a booth.
- Learn the "Break" of the woodwind instruments. The tone tends to change as your cross the "Break" so keep it in mind when writing melodies. Also avoid writing ostinatos that cross the "Break" it makes for very tricky fingerings.

Brass

- Consecutive long tones, especially at slower tempi cause fatigue. If you don't give your players breaks, either in how you write your cues by creating tacet measures every once in a while, or by recording long cues in several parts with pickups, you're more likely to encounter

Preparing for Scoring Sessions

problems that will slow you down. Keep in mind that the lower instruments require more breath, therefore they can't hold notes as long as trumpets can.
- Playing high notes softly is nearly impossible. Writing like that will lead to problems.
- Clean entrances in the high register are very difficult even if the dynamic is loud. Having a short ramp up into high notes is much easier.
- When using trumpets to support high strings, have them play an octave lower rather than unison. Playing up high in unison with strings is difficult.
- Anything above a high C is going to be difficult to achieve consistently.
- Brass can get very loud and quickly overwhelm the rest of the orchestra. If recording everyone together, consider the balance and dynamics in order to avoid problems.
- Key choices can make a huge difference to playability, it can be the difference between a tricky combination of embouchure, air pressure and fingering vs. much easier open piston positions and embouchure/pressure control. For example, playing in Ab Major is much harder than G.
- Legato interval leaps from notes in the staff to notes above the staff are very challenging. Even when tonguing, these leaps can be difficult to perform well consistently. Descending leaps are easier, but depending on the interval and key, may still be practically impossible without tonguing.
- Repeated fast double and triple tonguing is challenging. Ta da da da da da da da da da da da, is much harder, or possibly impossible vs. Ta da dum, Ta da dum, Ta da

dum...

- When using mutes, make sure there is ample time to insert, remove and change mutes. Trombones, and Tuba need more time than Trumpet. Failing to allow enough time will likely result in needing a pickup, which will slow down your session.

Percussion

- Percussionists lay out their instruments over stations and need time to move from one station to the next. Make sure you leave enough time for your player(s) to switch stations to reach the instruments they need to play.
- Save time and frustration by making complete perc parts for each player, rather than different parts per instrument. That way they can have copies at different stations and it's easier to follow and perform.
- Sorting out perc can be tricky, running things by a professional percussionist before the session can help prepare and plan how to station instruments in the most efficient layout for your music.
- Dead strokes, dampening and bowing can't be performed as quickly as other techniques. Keep this in mind when writing for perc.
- If writing for rare or unusual percussion instruments, make sure they are available, or that you have acceptable substitutes in case they aren't.
- Don't get too picky about describing mallets (i.e. "medium soft cord with birch handle" is too specific). If you have a specific request for a specific reason, it's best to

indicate that so the player can choose the appropriate mallet (i.e. "harder mallets, bring out more fundamental"). The latter direction lets the player know what you're after and they'll know how best to achieve it.

Piano

- If your piece sits in a key for a length of time, consider breaking tradition and use a key signature. Pianists are processing so much information and sightreading so much compared to single-line instruments, particularly with a tonal center that would normally have a key signature of many flats or sharps, it is unnecessarily taxing on a pianist to have to process accidentals bar after bar.
- Most pianists can reach a 9th, or even a 10th. However, if there are additional notes lying in between, their hand span won't reach as far. Large spans should be avoided in fast tempi, especially if there is no time to prepare to find the chord or interval.
- Unless you're after an unintuitive use of pedals, like intentionally blurring harmonies, don't include pedal markings, they will clutter the part. Just indicate "con pedale" and trust your pianist to decide where to use the pedal.
- Repeated notes can be easy to bow on a string or strike on a marimba, but much harder to play on piano, especially at fast tempi.
- If you place the piano in an isolation booth while recording with orchestra, make sure the pianist has a good line of sight to the conductor, as well as a way to communicate with the conductor and control booth. A bar counter like the ones provided to the rest of the musicians is

- appreciated. Neglecting these will cause delays if the pianist needs to communicate with the conductor or composer.
- While sometimes a piano may be programmed with the right and left hand separately, the two (or more) voices support each other and inform how the other is voiced, therefore the pianist should play both together. The only exception might be if the two hands are playing virtuosic and unrelated parts, in which case the pianist may request to split them.

Harp

- Harps use 7 pedals to set the scale in which they play. When writing chromatic passages, make sure they are playable and keep in mind the time it takes to switch pedal positions. If your piece is very chromatic, consider using 2 harps.
- There are differing schools of thought on harp markings. Generally, if you're unsure, it's best not to include pedal markings, let the player figure out how they prefer to do things. On the other hand, some will appreciate having well thought out pedal markings, and can always ignore them if they disagree. When in doubt, ask your player ahead of time if possible.
- When using the harp as a motor, it really helps to set up a pattern that is not constantly changing every beat so that the harpist is secure in playing it without the stress of having to read each and every note.
- Playing continual upbeats for a long time is impractical without have a strong downbeat to play every bar, or

Preparing for Scoring Sessions

- two. Otherwise, it can be a problem staying absolutely in time.
- If clicks are not being used, a harpist has to look away from the music to see the strings, especially in the high register, then watch the music and the conductor. Don't write something incredibly difficult that has to be sightread on the spot without some advance preparation.
- Unlike the piano, harpists only use 4 fingers as the pinkie is not long enough to reach the string without disturbing the correct hand position.

Choir

- Writing in phrasing/breathing is a huge help and will save a lot of time in the studio. Breathing is always a big part of the equation, so try singing your piece and seeing where the breaths naturally go. If you want staggered breathing, specify. Otherwise, indicate breath marks, slurs, and rests exactly where you want the lifts. On slower tempos, it's common for these to be on eighth rests.
- Clearly write out what vowels you want (ooh, OH, AH, Awe). You can write in adjectives to help guide your singers.
- If you have a made-up language or random syllables, spell them phonetically so your singers will sing them exactly as written. Specify if you want Latin vowels or any uncommon consonants in your notes.
- Common terms used to describe the choral style you're after (for film scores): Pure, Boy Soprano, Breathy, Young,

Classical, Light, Shimmery, Epic, Dramatic, Full-voiced, Edgy, Brassy, Chesty, Carmina Burana, Straight Tone, Dark, Bright, Nasal, Gutteral… any adjectives to help the choir get the tone/color you want is very helpful and saves time.
- Unlike most instrumental parts where only their part is on the page, singers prefer to see all vocal parts when they perform.
- Consistently write your middle part splits for SSA/SAA or TTB/TBB instead of unnecessarily doubling the middle notes on multiple staves.
- Be mindful of tessitura/range and dynamics with your vowels. Open vowels like AH and OH are much easier on loud dynamics, whereas a closed vowel like "oooh" or even a hum will work well on quiet moments. Singers love experimenting, so come into your sessions ready to try a few options out.
- In general, if you take a moment to sing through your piece, you'll discover what feels most natural with vowels, dynamics, phrasing, tone, etc. allowing you to effectively communicate all of these on the score.

Other Considerations

- If you have particularly challenging parts, it's a good idea to send them to the musicians ahead of time to give them the opportunity to practice ahead of time. This can save a lot of time on the session.
- Sometimes you may have a crew filming part of your session for a behind-the-scenes video. If that's the case, you'll want to plan to record featured cues when the

Preparing for Scoring Sessions

- crew is scheduled to be there.
- Similarly, your director or a producer may have limited availability to be at the sessions. It's usually best to make sure you're recording important cues when they're there, and less important ones when they're not.
- Occasionally, especially if you're doing a single session, some of your players may be rushing off to a different afternoon or evening session at a different studio. If this is the case, you may want to re-consider your original planned recording order since you could lose key players at the session's planned end who won't be available for overtime if needed. For example, you may have programmed a cue with a violin solo for the end of your session, but if you might lose your concertmaster if you go late, it's smart to re-arrange the order so the solo is recorded earlier in the session, and lower priority cues can be pushed further back. That way if you lose a few players, you can still get a good result with a smaller section as you go into overtime.

Sample Recording Order

Below is a sample recording order that I prepared for recording the score to Stargirl season 1 episode 112. I usually do these in Excel, and I include my own notes on the margins, which I don't print out when sending list to all involved. I only print the columns from Order to Notes, not the running time or my shorthand notes, which I use to help me pick the recording order. Copies of the record order go to the composer, recording engineer, recordist, music editor, stage manager, and conductor. I always have at least

2 or 3 extra copies on hand as sometimes the contractor or a producer or music executive might want one.

Notice I like to color code each hour of recording, which I find helps keep track of whether we are on, behind, or ahead of schedule as we record. If working overseas where there is just a single break during a 3-hour session I'll use just 2 shades, one for the 1st half and the 2nd half of the session.

Preparing for Scoring Sessions

	Stargirl 112						
	Strings – Sept 21, 2019 AM						
Order	Cue No.	Cue Name	Dur.	Notes			
1	1m09	Machine Test	3:21		3:21	Tension Drama	
2	1m04	Small Complication	1:02		4:23	Tension Drama	
3	1m19	Team Enters Lair	0:39	Strings only	5:02	Tension Drama	
4	1m10	It's Going to Work	0:38		5:40	Tension Drama	
5	1m00	Recap	0:58		6:38	Tension Drama	
6	1m02B	Crock & Tigress vs. The Dugans Pt. 2	1:39		8:17	Action	
7	1m20	ISA Manifesto	3:15		11:32	Action Drama	
8	1m13	Courtney & Mike On Portch	1:01	Strings only	12:33	Emotional	
9	104m30	Yolanda Is Wildcat	1:11		13:44	Emotional/Heroic	
10	1m11-12	Pat Was Right	2:46		16:30	Hourman Emotional	
11	1m17	Making a Plan	2:41		19:11	Hourman Drama	
12	1m16	Pat & Rick Crack Code	1:01	Strings only	20:12	Hourman Emotional	
13	1m07	Going to Cabin	0:54		21:06	Hourman Emotional	
14	1m06	Violin Story Pt. 2	0:23	3 violins only	21:29	Last	

	Brass – Sept 21, 2019 PM					
1	1m09	Machine Test	2:32			
2	1m00	Recap	0:58		3:30	
3	1m02B	Crock & Tigress vs. The Dugans Pt. 2	1:23		4:53	
4	1m20	ISA Manifesto	3:15		8:08	
5	1m17	Making a Plan	2:41		10:49	
6	1m07	Going to Cabin	0:56		11:45	
7	1m04	Small Complication	0:18	Horns & Bones	12:03	
8	1m10	It's Going to Work	0:24	Horns & Bones	12:27	
9	104m30	Yolanda Is Wildcat	0:43	Horns & Bones	13:10	
10	1m11-12	Pat Was Right	1:05	Horns only	14:15	

Part Five
Stem Considerations

These days, it's expected when delivering music to a dub stage to provide mix stems. With few exceptions, the days of just delivering a full mix to the final dub are behind us. So how do we decide how many stems to deliver, in what format(s), and what belongs in which stems? There are several considerations to keep in mind when making these decisions.

- Dub stage considerations.
- Mix considerations.
- Bass management.
- Editorial considerations.
- Musical Control.
- Dub Stage Considerations

Preparing for Scoring Sessions

It's important to have discussions with the re-recording mixer who will be receiving the materials early, certainly before you start the final mix. Find out the stage specs and their setup and track capacity. Providing more stems than the stage can handle will cause problems. On big budget projects, the track count seems unlimited, but it isn't. It's not uncommon to combine the dialog/ADR tracks with the music tracks into a single session and I've been on tentpole films on major stages where we've maxed out the voice count. On lower budget projects all the sound including effects, Foley, dialog, and music may all get imported into a single session, meaning even less available voices for music stems.

It may make sense to provide more stems to a 3-4 week mix on a major feature film than to a 1-day mix of a TV episode because of the speed at which those mixers must work. The more time there is to mix, the more attention the mixer will be able to give the stems. The less time there is, the less likely the mixer is going to even consider the stems.

Keep in mind that generally re-recording mixers will group all the stems onto a single fader and only make adjustments to the stems if there are sonic issues that arise, or to address notes that cannot be effectively addressed globally without adjusting the stems.

Mix Considerations

The more stems you require, the more complex the music mix becomes, which sometimes can affect how many days your mixer needs to complete the task. Another consideration is that the more stems you have, the more opportunities for mistakes there are, meaning quality control is a bit more challenging and time consuming.

It's good to discuss the stem formats with your re-recording and scoring mixers if possible. Some mixers like to print all stems in the same format, i.e. 5.1 or 7.1 or 7.1.2 stems for everything, even if some of them only have audio data on the LCR channels, or have no sub. They like the consistency. Others prefer to print each stem in the format that makes most sense for that stem i.e. choir might only be 5.0, Percussion might be LCR, other stems might be in quad format. I've even seen mixers that print all stems without any sub information and then print 1 or 2 dedicated sub stems. In my experience most re-recording mixers will accept whatever format the mixer chooses, but it never hurts to have a conversation about it early on, which could help streamline things. I prefer stems that are in the format that makes sense for the stem rather than all stems being the same whether all channels are used or not. It seems like a waste of voices to have 7.1.2 stems for something that only has information in the LCR, and visually when editing it's not as comfortable to look at as simply looking at an LCR stem.

Here's an example of a stem that only uses 5 channels printed as 7.1 above, and 5.0 below. At the same track size, you can see the wave forms are easier to read in the 5.0 version than the 7.1 version where they are smaller and compressed because of the 3 empty channels that need to fit in the same space.

Preparing for Scoring Sessions

Here's an example of the same, but this time it's using just 4 channels comparing what it looks like in a 7.1 stem above, or quad stem below.

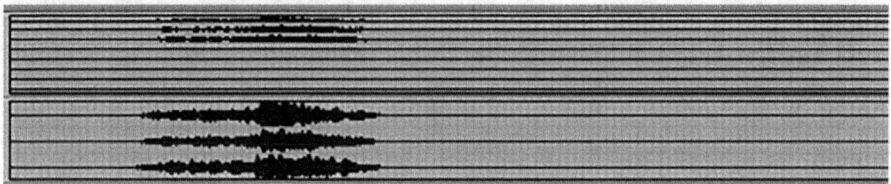

And here's one more, this time comparing 3 channels in a 7.1 stem above vs. an LCR stem below.

As you can see, the fewer empty channels are in a stem, the easier it is to read the wave file, which matters when editing the audio. This is why I prefer varying stem formats as appropriate for each stem rather than using the same single format for all stems, regardless of how many channels are being used.

The next, and most important of the mix considerations in my view, is the sonic quality of the music and what stems make creative sense to provide the final dub. What I mean by this is that if there are sounds that are more likely to compete with sound effects than others, you probably want to separate those into a stem. That way if they do clash with other frequencies in the sound effects or dialog or anything else, the re-recording mixer can just lower or EQ or otherwise address that stem, while leaving the rest of the stems alone. If those sounds are married to other sounds, then the re-recording mixer has no choice but to lower everything. A good example is separating brass from the rest of the orchestra, if possible, because sometimes brass can become a little bright or overpowering in context with all other sound. When it's on its own stem, the re-recording can just tuck in or EQ the brass a little bit, while keeping the rest of the orchestra as delivered. However, if the entire orchestra is on a single stem, they will have no choice but to lower or EQ the entire orchestra, which could reduce the efficacy or impact of the music.

Consider what types of sounds you're using in your score, and what makes sense to potentially split out into separate stems to give a re-recording mixer control to maximize the impact of the score. Another important consideration is any director notes where s/he might have misgivings about certain musical elements. It's not uncommon for a director to give a note while listening to demos, or during recording sessions along the lines of "I'm not 100% sure about that flute solo." I don't mean to pick on my flutist friends, it could be any instrument, synth, or sample, I just picked flute for example's sake because it's something I have literally heard a director say on a score I once worked on. If there are any notes like this, make sure the flagged elements are on their own stem so they can be raised, lowered, or even muted if necessary.

Bass Management

This is really a variant of mix considerations, but I think it's important enough to warrant its own section within this chapter. Bass management is often an issue that comes up when mixing, be it the music mix, or the final dub. I think using formats that have

Preparing for Scoring Sessions

a sub track is fine (i.e. 5.1, 7.1, 7.1.2), and there's no need to create dedicated sub tracks (i.e. 5.0 or 7.0 and a separate mono sub track). I actually prefer not having a dedicated sub track because dedicated sub tracks tend to mix sub information from several stems, while stems with a .1 sub track stay together with their respective stems and the dub stage can easily manage that sub track for each stem. However, when a score has pre-records that include synths, or electric bass I like to have a bass stem where all the pre-record bass or low end non percussive sounds live. This is very convenient on the dub stage because all the low frequency information of those types of sounds is in one place.

Editorial Considerations

In addition to mix considerations, keep in mind editorial considerations. If you're working on a locked picture and don't expect any conforms will be necessary, you may not need as many stems as when you're working on a film where the picture continues to change after scoring, as is often the case. If you're expecting the music will have to be editorially conformed after the mix, providing your music editor good stems can allow them more options and freedom to create better edits than if they have less stems, or no stems. As a music editor I've worked on films where I literally had to create new cues when a director decided the cue a composer wrote wasn't working for a scene, and having sufficient stems allowed me to creatively take elements from different cues to create something new that addressed the director's notes. When I worked on Krypton and Stargirl, certain characters had themes that also had a very specific sonic signature, and we'd always print those on their own stems. This allowed me a lot of flexibility when tracking cues in subsequent episodes, or if the showrunner asked "can we add the brainwave theme here?" Having that on its own stem meant I could quickly find other cues that had that theme, find one in an appropriate tempo and key and add it to whatever was there rather than having to try and cut a completely new cue.

Musical Control

As I described above, I've had to get extremely creative on occasion and rework or literally create new cues using stems on the dub stage. However, consider how much control your stems are giving your music editor and the re-recording mixer. I have experienced situations where having lots of stems has enabled others to rework the score to such an extent that the composer was unhappy with the result. Heck, it happened to me on an early indie film I scored, where the re-recording mixer decided to literally remix the music to his tastes rather than maintaining the integrity of the mixes I provided. If you're working with inexperienced people, or with people you might not know well or trust, you may want to limit the amount of stems you provide them as a way of limiting how much they can change.

Stem Layout

There is no standard stem layout, and each project will lead to a different layout based on the variables mentioned above. That said here are some recommendations that I have found to be very useful over the years.

Preparing for Scoring Sessions

Instrument Sections

When recording sections separately, having strings and woodwinds together often works well. This is true both during the recording, or even if recorded separately combining the two into a single stem usually works well. Often the woodwinds are orchestrated to provide support to the strings, so this makes sense.

Separating the brass to its own stem if it was recorded separately is recommended. If you record orchestral percussion, many mixers prefer to have the timpani recorded on its own. Recording metals separately than drums or mallets can also be useful. All these elements may end up combined into a single orchestral perc stem in the mix, but not always. It's not uncommon to see a Metals stem, a Mallets or Pitched Perc stem and an Orchestral Perc stem (assuming things were recorded separately). Hi Perc and Low Perc, or even Hi, Mid, and Low Perc stems are other common ways of printing those.

Choir

Choir should always be on its own stem if possible.

Solo vocals

Most often solo vocals will be on their own stem. However sometimes they can comfortably live in the choir stem depending on what's happening musically.

Piano

Many composers provide a PBH (Piano, Bells, Harp) stem. I prefer to separate the piano and have it on its own dedicated stem. Depending on the style of the music I might have the harp and bells on a single stem, or I've had occasion to put the harp on a mallet stem, where musically what the harp was doing was mirroring or complementing the mallets.

Keys

Some scores feature a lot of keyboards, or perhaps a mix of keyboards and piano. As long as the keys and piano make sense together, I may just have a keys stem instead of a piano stem and print all keys and piano together. Sometimes the sonic quality or musical function of the keys is significantly different than the piano, in which case I'll have a piano stem and a keys stem.

Guitars

If a score features guitars, I'll usually have a guitar stem. I recently worked on a score that had lots of rhythm guitars as well as guitars playing melodies. I ended up having 2 guitar stems, one for the rhythm stuff and another for the melodic stuff. Ukulele, mandolin, banjo, dulcimers and other strummed instruments can often share the same stem, again it depends on the what's happening musically. On occasion I've had harp on the guitar stem when there was no need for a dedicated harp stem, and it made musical sense.

Non Orchestral Percussion

Depending on the nature of the music it may be beneficial to have a metallic perc stem and a non-metallic perc stem. Other times it may be beneficial to have Hi and Low Perc stems, or even Hi, Mid and Low as described above. Again, the decision is driven by the style of the music and how much control you wish to provide

Preparing for Scoring Sessions

to the dub stage.

Synths

I usually separate pads, atmospheres, and moving synths like pulsing or arpeggiating synths. If a score features synth leads, those might end up on a separate stem, too. Sometimes a piano might be doubled by a synth to change the color of the piano. In cases like that I'll often have that synth printed on the piano stem since they go together.

Unusual/ethnic instruments

If your score features unusual instruments, it often makes sense to create a separate stem for those.

Other (sometimes called Extra)

I always have at least one stem called Other. This gives me the flexibility to move things around when the music dictates it. For example, I may have strings and woodwinds together, but on one particular cue there's an oboe solo that I could imagine wanting to either bring out even more during the dub, or perhaps the reverse, so I'll put this on the Other stem. If after setting my stem layout I find some cues using instruments or sounds that don't neatly fit into any other stem, I'll put them on the Other stem. When I worked on Stargirl, there were specific sounds that were associated with specific characters, I had 2 Other stems and always put those sounds in the Other tracks so we always had the ability to raise or lower those specific sounds. It also helped with editing as described above.

If you have a score that doesn't require a lot of stems, but there is a guitar on just one or two cues, or some other instrument that only appears sporadically, having an Other stem is a great way to have those instruments on their own stems without creating dedicated stems that will be empty more often than not., For example if there is a vocal solo in just a handful of places it may not be worth having a dedicated Solo Vox stem and it can live in the Other stem instead.

Generally, my approach is to create the fewest stems that are necessary to provide the level of control that's appropriate for the project. Whatever your stem layout, always include a Clicks stem and a Full Mix stem. If you're working in formats that are wider than just stereo, also provide a Full Stereo Mix.

Sample Stem Layouts

The following is the stem layout used on one of my TV shows, all stems were stereo:

- 01 Strings
- 02 Brass
- 03 Choir
- 04 Guitars
- 05 Perc
- 06 Pads
- 07 Rhythmic Synths
- 08 Other
- 09 Full Mix

Here's the layout from a different TV show, again all stereo stems:

Preparing for Scoring Sessions

```
01   Orch
02   Brass
03   Keys
04   Loops
05   Perc Loops
06   Drums
07   Bass
08   Other 1
09   Other 2
10   Other 3
11   Full Mix
```

Here's an example from a low budget documentary feature, all stems were stereo:

```
01   Solos
02   Solo Strings
03   Orch
04   Piano
05   Vox
06   Pads
07   Pulse
08   Bass
09   Other
10   Full Mix
```

Here's an example from a medium budget documentary feature, all stems were 5.1 unless otherwise indicated:

```
01   Clicks (mono stem)
02   Strings
```

03 Solo Strings (the sub channel was left empty)
04 Drums
05 Perc
06 Piano (the sub channel was left empty)
07 Keys
08 Pads
09 Pulse (the sub channel was left empty)
10 Rhythm Guitars (only the LCR channels were used, the others were left empty)
11 Melodic Guitars (only the LCR channels were used, the others were left empty)
12 Bass
13 Other
14 5.1 Full Mix
15 Stereo Mix (stereo stem)

Here's an example from a medium-budget feature:

01 Strings 5.0 stem
02 Brass 5.0 stem
03 Traditional Winds 5.0 Stems
04 Plucks 5.0 stem
05 Guitars LCR stem
06 Synths 1 5.1 stem (sub channel wasn't always used, depending on the sounds)
07 Synths 2 5.1 stem (sub channel wasn't always used, depending on the sounds)
08 Traditional Perc Hi LCR stem
09 Traditional Perc Low 5.1 stem
10 Orch Perc LCR + sub printed on a 5.1 stem

Preparing for Scoring Sessions

11   Pitched Perc 5.0 stem
12   Jaw Harp 5.0 stem
13   Extra 1 5.1 stem (sounds used for each cue determined how many channels were utilized)
14   Extra 2 5.1 stem (sounds used for each cue determined how many channels were utilized)
15   Extra 3 5.1 stem (sounds used for each cue determined how many channels were utilized)
16   5.1 Mix 5.1 stem
17   Stereo Mix stereo stem
18   Clicks mono stem

And finally, here's an example from a big budget feature the orchestral stems were 7.1.2 all other stems were 7.1 whether the sub channel was used or not.

01   Click
02   Strings/Winds
03   Brass
04   Orch FX
05   Choir
06   Solos
07   Perc Metals
08   PBH (Piano, Bells, Harp)
09   Perc Drums
10   Synth Short
11   Synth Arps
12   Synth Pads
13   Synth Lead
14   Synth Special

15 Guitars
16 Bass
17 Hits/Transitions
18 Sub Booms
19 Extra 1
20 Extra 2
21 Extra 3
22 7.1.2 Full Mix
23 Stereo Mix

As you can see from these examples, stem layouts can vary quite a bit, however there are commonalities, and as described above, it's all about what makes sense in terms of the final mix & editorial needs for the project.

Preparing for Scoring Sessions

A Guide for Media Composers and Their Teams

Part Six
Pro Tools Session Prep

This may be obvious but in the interest of being thorough and for anyone who has little or no experience recording live instruments here's a quick overview of the process. When recording live instruments, whether remote recording soloists who record themselves at home, or a full orchestra on a scoring stage, you'll need to prepare materials for the recording sessions. In addition to scores and parts, you'll typically create Pro Tools sessions for the recording engineer to work with. Each cue gets its own session. Unless you're recording free time with no click and no pre-records, each session should have the MIDI meter and tempo map imported and lined up at the correct timecode to be in sync with picture, clicks, the mockup, picture (QuickTime file), and all pre-records organized by the stems to which they will eventually be printed to. If what you're recording isn't to picture, you'll follow the same steps except you won't need to provide or link to a

Preparing for Scoring Sessions

QuickTime file.

The recording engineer (or his/her assistant) will import his/her empty tracks on which the instruments will be recorded into the session you provide, along with any aux tracks, master tracks or whatever else they use when recording. Once the recording is done those sessions will be prepared for the score mix and used to mix the music.

Generally speaking, I advocate for preparing sessions in such a way that they are ready for both the recording sessions, and the mix. That way once the live tracks are added they can go straight to the mix with no further adjustments other than comping takes. This keeps things streamlined and efficient. However, sometimes this isn't possible, or due to circumstances it may not be the best approach. For example, when doing remote recordings and there are lots of pre-records, it might be more efficient to create mix-minus stems to send to the recording sessions, and then add all the prerecords after recording, when preparing the sessions for the mix. This is especially true when hiring soloists to home-record themselves. More on these scenarios in the next section. In this section we'll focus on what I think is the ideal workflow, meaning preparing everything for a scoring stage so it can be used both for recording and mixing.

A Guide for Media Composers and Their Teams

Printing Pre-Records

Before you can build your Pro Tools sessions, you need to have your composer provide all the pre-records and/or guides as well as a reference mix (aka mockup). You want to make sure that they print all pre-records, so they begin at Bar 1 and all end at the same place, even if it means plenty of empty space within the file. When importing them into Pro Tools as described below, this makes it clear that everything is in order. Getting tracks of varying lengths raises questions, why aren't they all matching? Is that intentional or a mistake? That's why it's good practice to make sure all tracks are the same length.

This screenshot is an example of what the Pro Tools session will look like when the files are of varying lengths, I recommend avoiding this method.

Preparing for Scoring Sessions

In this next screenshot you see an example of what the Pro Tools session will look like when the same pre-records are all printed at the same duration. This is the recommended method.

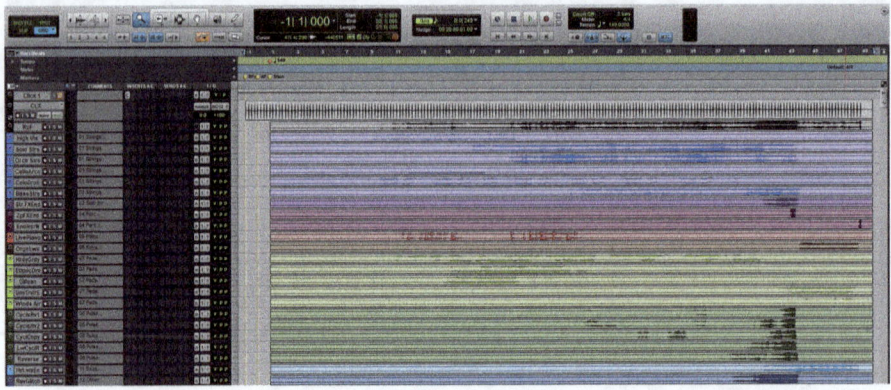

As you can see, in the second image it's clear everything was printed from beginning to end, and having a block of tracks that line up looks better than the first image where tracks end at varying durations. In the first example there's no easy way to confirm that indeed that's where the track was supposed to end. There's no way of knowing if perhaps there was more audio later that accidentally didn't get printed.

I'd like to reiterate the importance of printing everything starting at bar 1. When you export your MIDI the MIDI file you create will always start at Bar 1. Even if you're working with negative bars or your music begins at bar 3 or bar 5, MIDI files don't retain that information and will always start at Bar 1. I highly encourage you not to use negative bars, and always have your sequence start at bar 1. It's quite common for the music to start at bar 3 or later, and that's fine. This way, when you export your MIDI the bar numbers will match what's in your DAW, and printing your audio from bar

1 means where the MIDI and the audio begins is the same. If you're on a DAW that allows negative bars and love to use them, I encourage you to renumber your bars so they start at bar 1 before exporting your MIDI to avoid issues of bar numbers not lining up properly. The only real exception that I can see is if for some reason the music doesn't start until many bars into the MIDI meter map. Sometimes this can happen if during the composing process the composer and the director decide to delay where a cue begins. The composer may opt to simply leave empty bars in the beginning of the cue so s/he can just tweak the entrance at its new delayed location. This can make life easier in these types of circumstances and is perfectly acceptable. It may be silly to print a cue that starts at bar 1 when the music doesn't actually start until bar 30. While I think it's fine to have 29 empty bars if that's what happened, you can also opt to start printing at bar 27 or 29 in which case you should indicate this in the file names with something like "B27" at the end of the file name and make sure whomever is building the sessions is aware.

Filename Conventions

When printing your pre-records, it's important to properly name the audio files. You'll want to include the following information: Project name or code, cue number, cue name (optional), version number, picture version to which it was written, the start timecode for the audio file and what instrument is printed. Ideally you've got things setup correctly in your DAW so that when printing your pre-records they are correctly timestamped. This helps speed up the process when building Pro Tools sessions and is also a way to double check that things are in the right place by comparing the

Preparing for Scoring Sessions

timestamp to what's in the file name.

Here are some examples of good filenames:

MAP 1m01 Main Titles v2 p20221215 tc01000000 Violins 1.wav

1m01 MAP Main Titles v2 p20221215 tc01000000 Reference Mix.wav

2m12 v4.2 MAP The Kiss 20221215 2.15.47.07 - Bass Arp.wav

MAP_4m26v3_20221215_Speed_Monster_04070618.wav

Note in the first example I start with the project code, which is very common. "p20221215" indicates picture version 20221215 "tc01000000" indicates the start timecode is 01:00:00:00. The second example has the cue number first, which is my preferred approach. The third version doesn't bother with "p" to indicate it's the picture version and the timecode has dots between the hours, minutes, seconds and frames, which I find makes it easier to read and makes it obvious the first set of numbers are the picture version and the second set are the file's start timecode. I also like having a dash before the instrument name, I honestly don't know why, I just think it looks clear. The fourth example uses underscores instead of spaces. Personally, I don't like this and don't think it's necessary, but some people like it. Notice the version number and order of the information is different in each example. All of these are excellent filenames that provide all the necessary information in a clear way, so whichever way you prefer to do things is fine as long as all the information is in the filename.

Be consistent with your file naming conventions. Once you pick one way of doing it, make sure all your files follow the same style and are consistently labeled.

Creating Sessions

Create a folder labeled something like "Sessions for recording and mixing." This is where you'll create individual session folders for each cue. Label each session folder consistently. Don't use spaces for some names and underscores for others. Don't use CAPS in some places but not in others. Generally, I'm not a fan of CAPS except perhaps for project codes or to indicate Alternate versions or optional (i.e. ALT or OPT). The session folder names should at a minimum include the cue number. However, it's best practice to include the project name or code, along with cue number and you may want to also include the cue name and the cue version. For example, "My Awesome Project 1m01 Main Titles v2" or perhaps "MAP 1m01 Main Titles v2". I often prefer to start with the cue number and then the other information like this - "1m01 MAP Main Titles vs2". The reason I prefer the latter is that the cue numbers are the first thing in the name, meaning it's easy to quickly jump to cues by just typing the cue numbers, rather than having to use the mouse. That said, if I'm working with a composer who has his/her preferred naming conventions, as long as they're clear and include all the necessary information I follow their conventions.

Once you have your empty session, it's time to build it. I like to start with the cues that have the most pre-record tracks, so I can work out the stem layout that'll work best for the project. Sometimes I might look at 2 or 3 big cues to figure it out. Once I have my layout worked out, I can build all the sessions using that layout.

Importing Pre-records

Assuming the composer isn't working in Pro Tools already and delivers all of his/her pre-records as individual audio files, I usually start by dragging them into the session. This will automatically create tracks for each audio file and name the track with the audio file name. Next, assuming we're working to picture I'll spot the clips to the correct timecode. Ideally the audio files are timestamped, but if they aren't I'll manually move them to the correct timecode. If working on projects that are not synced to picture, I'll usually spot the clips to the beginning of the session. Most composers start writing at bar 3 or bar 5, so this works well. However, if the music begins exactly at Bar 1 I'll leave some free time ahead of the start of the clips in order to leave room for pre-roll and warning clicks instead of putting them at the beginning of the session.

Reference Mix

Your composer should always provide a reference mix, aka a mockup of each cue along with the pre-records. Make sure you import the mockup into your session and line it up correctly with the pre-records.

MIDI

Next, I import the MIDI file and line it up to the correct spot corresponding with the audio, so the tempo and meter maps are in the session. Usually this creates at least one, often many MIDI tracks, delete those, they are not needed, all we need is the meter and tempo maps. You should also clear the MIDI clips from the clip bin.

Clicks

Often your composer will also print a click track along with the pre-records and mockup. If that's the case, you can simply import their click track into the session. In the world of media recording, it's standard to use a UREI click sound with no accents. Alternatively, an MPC click sound can be used. If your composer's click track doesn't conform to these conventions or your composer doesn't provide a proper click track, you should create one.

There are a couple of ways to create a click track which I will describe here:

You can simply create a click track in Pro Tools using the built-in plug-in, select the UREI unaccented settings for both accented and unaccented clicks, set the output to a mono bus, then create a mono track and set the input to that same mono bus and simply record the click from beginning to end to create a click audio file. Don't forget to Name the file using your file naming convention as described above.

My preferred method is a little different. Years ago, I created a short audio file of a single UREI unaccented click. I create a mono track and set the timebase to ticks, and then I just copy/paste the individual click onto each beat on the gird. There's no need to literally paste each individual click, you can create one bar and then duplicate it over and over. What's cool about this is that if there are tempo changes, the clicks will follow those changes since your timebase is ticks. It's also really easy to manipulate odd meter bars like a 7/8 to decide how you want the clicks to play. And after doing this for my first cue, I simply import this track into

Preparing for Scoring Sessions

subsequent cues and the clicks automatically line up to the tempo map of the new cue. I just have to be careful if there are odd meter bars to make sure things are correct. If I have too many clicks I simply delete the excess clicks. If I need more, I simply duplicate more bars. And if I want I can simply consolidate the audio track into a single audio file after building the clicks so it looks just like as described above, though it's not really necessary.

Whichever method you chose to use, make sure to begin 2 bars before the music starts so you have the option to give one or two free bars of clicks before the musicians have to play. You should also trim the clicks so they stop when the cue ends, this will avoid any possible click blead from headphones into the microphones - this can particularly be an issue with quiet cues. If the cue ends with a staccato or strong hit on the downbeat of bar 40, my last click will be bar 40 beat 1. If the last bar is in 4/4 and the cue ends with a held note over the first 3 beats of the bar, the last beat will be the 4th beat of that bar. Finally, I like to leave in the built-in click track as a backup. Some recordists like to use that instead of printed clicks.

Track order

Next, I arrange the pre-records from top to bottom following the stem layout for the project. I prefer to have my stem layout follow score order, but I know many people have other preferences. It honestly doesn't really matter as long as it's consistent across sessions. Within each stem group, I order things in score order so for example woodwinds would be ordered with flutes on top, then oboes, then clarinets and finally bassoons. I then go one step

A Guide for Media Composers and Their Teams

further and arrange the order of the tracks based on where the audio on the track starts, with the earliest on top and the latest on the bottom. I do this for two reasons. First, I think it looks a little bit neater, second most mixers I know mix from the beginning to the end of a cue and listen to individual tracks one at a time, so having things ordered this way means they can simply go down the line.

In this screenshot you can see how I organized string pre-records as an example. Note there are often 2 sets of tracks for each instrument (usually for different articulations), and I order them by the one that plays first above the one that plays next. I then put ensemble tracks below.

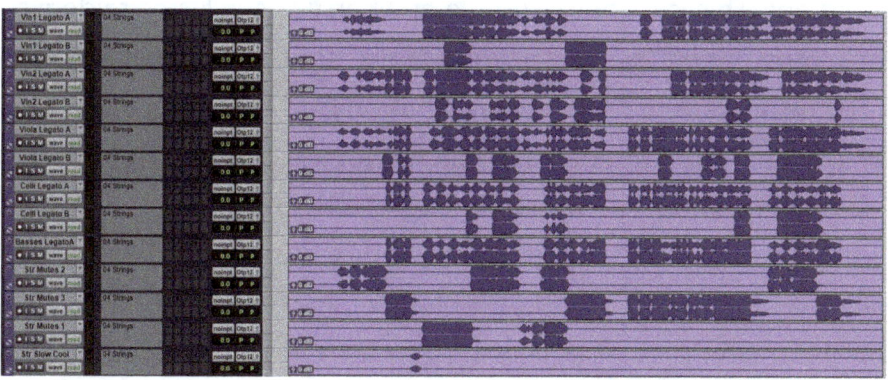

The following screenshot demonstrates how I order non orchestral instruments by the order in which they first appear, in this case it's High World Percussion, but I use this principle on everything..

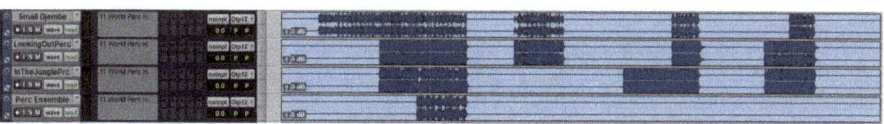

Admittedly taking the time to sort the tracks this way may

Preparing for Scoring Sessions

be overkill, but it doesn't take very long, and I think using this method keeps the sessions looking neat and organized, which the recipients appreciate.

Folders

Sometimes I'll use folders and put all tracks that belong to a particular stem in a folder. I don't usually do this unless there are a lot of tracks and then folders can be nice.

On occasion, especially when working on video games, cues may have layers that need to be stemmed out, such as High Intensity and Low Intensity, or Day and Night, or based on game locations. This is a good example of when I'll usually use folders to help organize my tracks. The main tracks that make up the base of the cue and are common to all variations are either not in a folder, or in a Main Tracks folder, then each layer will consist of a folder (or sub-folder) with its corresponding tracks, making it very clear what's what. Here's an example where you'll see that uses 2 versions of a cue. The tracks that are common to both versions are on the top level, then there's a folder for version 1 and a folder for version 2. Notice the color coding remains consistent with the stems (more on colors below), in this case when the mixer id done and prints the stems s/he will provide files indicating Pads version 1 and Pads version 2 as well as Pulse version 1 and Pulse version 2.

A Guide for Media Composers and Their Teams

Track names

Keep names short and informative. By default, the track names mirror the filenames that you dragged into the session. Often these are long and include the project name, cue number, timecode, picture version or other information. There are only so many letters that fit in the track name before Pro Tools condenses the names into gibberish. Furthermore, none of that additional info is necessary within the track name. All you need is an indication of what is on the track, i.e. "Flutes" or a patch name like "Alchemy" or "Harvest Moonz." You can use the batch renaming function to quickly and easily remove unnecessary information from the track names.

It's very helpful to keep track names consistent across different sessions for different cues. This makes it easy for the mixer to match tracks and import settings from one session to the next, which they commonly do. If the track names are inconsistent, the track matching function in the import window isn't as effective

Preparing for Scoring Sessions

and there's more manual labor involved.

Colors and Comments

I like to color-code tracks based on the stem they belong to. This is another visual aid that helps keep the session organized and easy to look at. It's important to keep the colors consistent between sessions.

I also like to indicate what stem each track belongs to in the comments. Each stem gets a number in addition to its name. This helps when printing the mixes because those numbers make sure everything stays in order across all cues. I do this for two reasons, first it's a way to double check that things are going where they should, and second, I worked with a color-blind colleague for whom colors alone weren't very helpful because they couldn't distinguish the difference between some of the different colors and they relied on the comments.

I usually have to do all this manually for the first cue, and as described above I like to start with the biggest couple of cues so I can work out my stem layout. Once the layout is set, the comments and colors are indicated, I will save the track settings for each stem, which I can then recall when building sessions for subsequent cues. This makes it easy to keep things consistent across sessions.

You can pick whichever colors you like, though I learned a cool method of picking colors from recording and mixing engineer Brad Haehnel that I like and have adopted. I start with the top left color in the color palette window for my first stem assignment, I think skip one column and select the bottom row color for the next stem assignment, then I skip a column and go back to the top row color and continue to alternate this way as you can see in this screenshot.

If I have more stems and need even more colors, I reverse the process until I run out of stems as you can see in the next screenshot.

Counter & Rulers

When preparing your sessions, make sure your counter and rulers are set correctly. Set the main counter to **Bars | Beats** and the sub counter to **Timecode**. As for your rulers, you'll want to display **Bars|Beats, Timecode, Tempo** and **Meter**. If you use markers, display the Markers ruler, too.

Preparing for Scoring Sessions

Check the Scores

Finally, before I share the sessions with anyone, I check them against the scores to make sure the tempo and meter maps match up. Sometimes orchestrators will re-meter cues for better readability. Usually they'll alert you, but they are human and can sometimes forget, or I might miss a note in an email and not realize they did it. If there are differences between the score and the session, I'll confirm which is correct and then remeter the session to match the score, or if the score is wrong, I'll alert the orchestrators so they can correct it.

This step is also a quality control step. On rare occasions I've found discrepancies between a session and its corresponding score, which led us to discover that the orchestrator was sent a different version of a cue. In those cases, we'll investigate to see who has the correct version and we can then update whoever needs to be updated. Better to catch it now than on the scoring stage.

Here are screenshots of a sample session that's ready to go to the scoring stage. Due to the track count there are 2 pages.

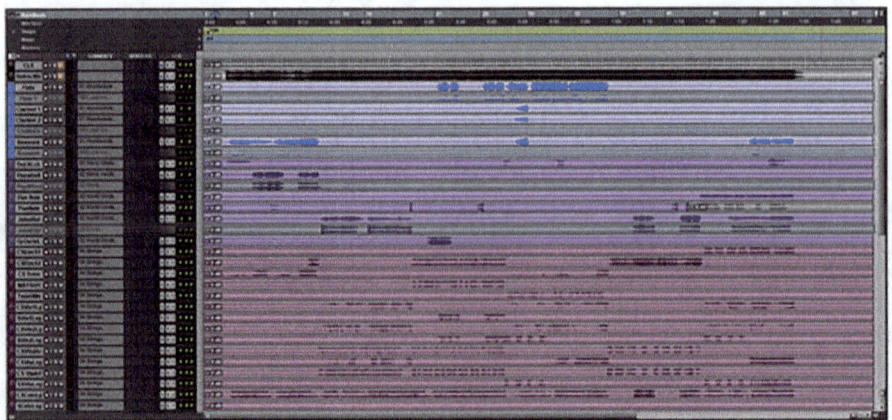

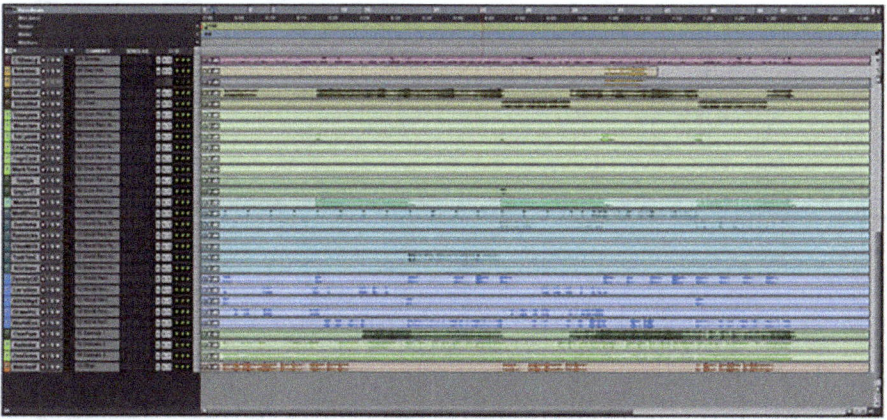

You may notice some muted tracks that seem to mirror the tracks directly above them. The unmuted mono tracks are soloist pre-records we recorded via remote sessions in advance. The muted stereo tracks are the samples that were replaced by the soloists. I leave them in the session in case the composer or the mixer wants to refer to them at any time.

Preparing for Scoring Sessions

A Guide for Media Composers and Their Teams

Part Seven
Remote Recording

In the previous section I went into detail about how I like to prepare Pro Tools sessions for the recording and mix stage. However, sometimes when doing remote recordings this approach isn't practical or preferable. In this section I'll discuss some differences when doing remote recordings that may affect how you would want to prepare your materials.

To Pro Tools or Not to Pro Tools

While not new, ever since the pandemic, most professional musicians seem to have a home recording setup these days. While some use Pro Tools as their DAW, others do not. For those who do not, a Pro Tools session is no help at all. In such cases, they'll want audio files and a MIDI file instead. Sending countless pre-record tracks won't do. Instead, you'll want to print a mix-minus

Preparing for Scoring Sessions

for whichever instrument is being recorded. Even if they do use Pro Tools, sending lots of audio files can be cumbersome with long upload and download times, and not necessary.

Find Out What They Want

Considering the above, it's good to find out what the recipient wants, a Pro Tools session? Individual files? Complete stems, or a mix minus? I've worked with remote orchestras where instead of sending pre-record tracks I sent a session with 2 or three different mix-minuses to match the different sections we were recording (i.e. mix minus strings, mix minus brass).

What to Send

If you're sending a simple Pro Tools session, all the details I described above apply, except instead of having lots of pre-record tracks you'll simply have mix minus stems as appropriate. I also recommend adding guide stems of just what's being recorded so that if one plays the mix-minus + the guide they hear the full mix. This is especially useful when working with soloists, it allows them to isolate just their part as you've mocked it up for a better reference of what you're after. Here's an example from a recent vocal session I did with a singer who uses Pro Tools. All I sent was a Mix-minus and the sample vocal reference track. Since the tempo is steady throughout we just used the built-in click track and didn't bother to print clicks.

If you're not sending a Pro Tools session, but instead sending individual files, here's what you'll want to send:

A Guide for Media Composers and Their Teams

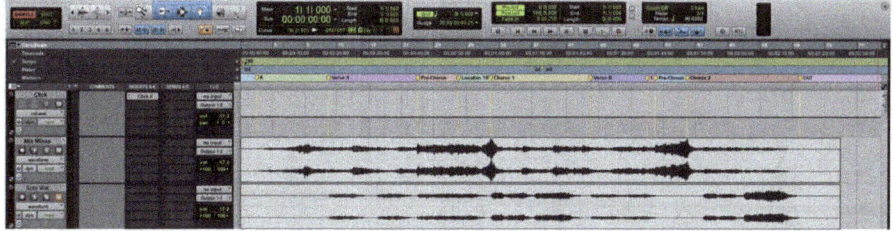

- Reference mix (aka Mockup)
- Mix minus (if recording multiple instruments, there may be multiple mix minuses, one for each instrument)
- Individual guides (as described above, one for each instrument being recorded)
- Click track
- MIDI file
- PDF part(s)

Again, you want to make sure that all your audio files begin at Bar 1. That way everything will line up properly and there is no room for mistakes on the part of the recipient. WAV files are standard, make sure they are in whatever sample and bit rate you're using in your project, and make sure the recipient knows what those settings should be.

In my experience, I've never sent picture to soloists, it's usually not necessary. But if it is, consult the previous section regarding sending video.

Preparing for Scoring Sessions

A Guide for Media Composers and Their Teams

Part Eight
File Naming Conventions

Clear and consistent file names help minimize mistakes and keep things clear. In this section I'll review some suggested conventions that are highly recommended. Some of this was covered earlier, but I think it deserves its own section.

When working on music for visual media, you'll want to make sure to include the following within your file names:

- Project name or code
- Cue number
- Cue name (optional, I prefer to include it)
- Cue version number
- Picture version to which the cue syncs up
- Start timecode (the start timecode should be where the audio file starts, not where the music starts, and the

Preparing for Scoring Sessions

        file's timestamp should match)
- Indication of what the track is (i.e. Mockup, Stereo Mix, Reference, pre-record, or stem).

For example, "1m01 MAP Main Titles v3 P20221214 TC 1.03.14.12 Mockup"

The P stands for Picture followed by the picture version as indicated in the video file. Many people don't bother with dots between the hours, minutes, seconds, and frames of the timecode so it may look like this "1m01 MAP Main Titles P20221214 TC 1031412 Ref." I find it easier to read the timecode with the dots and they don't seem to be problematic on either on Mac or Windows operating systems.

If you're labeling a pre-record called "Sparkle" for example, your file name should look like this:

"1m01 MAP Main Titles P20221214 TC 1.03.14.12 Sparkle" Some people like to add a dash before the track name like this "1m01 MAP Main Titles v3 P20221214 TC 1.03.14.12 - Sparkle" both are fine.

If you're labeling a mix stem, make sure you include the stem number and name. This will help confirm that when importing the stems will always line up in the correct order:

"1m01 MAP Main Titles v3 P20221214 TC 1.03.14.12 - 01 Strings"

or

"1m01 MAP Main Titles v3 P20221214 TC 1.03.14.12 - 05 Pads"

Many mixers like to add their initials and the mix version at the end, too. For example, if your music is mixed by Noah Scot Snyder you might see:

1m01 MAP Main Titles v3 P20221214 TC 1.03.14.12 - 12 Full Mix NSS01

This way if there are mix revisions it's abundantly clear which version you're working with.

Consistency in file naming is key. If you sometimes begin with the cue number, but other times begin with the show code, things won't sort correctly in your folders. If you sometimes use underscores and other times spaces, you'll have the same issue. If you're inconsistent with CAPS things won't look as clear. The more consistency, the less questions, the smoother and more efficiently things will work.

Preparing for Scoring Sessions

A Guide for Media Composers and Their Teams

Addendum One
Score Mix

While this booklet focuses on preparing for recording sessions, the final step after recording is mixing and delivering the score to the dub stage, which has been mentioned throughout this booklet to some extent. It's critical to consider this early when planning and setting things up. I would be remiss not to touch on these topics in a bit more detail, which I cover in this and the next Addendum sections.

Mix Budget

Below is a sample mix budget comparison for the above recordings described in Part 2 (60 minutes). This assumes mixing for 8 days, that's a rate of roughly 8 minutes a day (7.5 days + .5 day for printing stems). I'm also assuming the mix happens in London or Los Angeles regardless of where the scoring took place.

Preparing for Scoring Sessions

	Low budget	Mid budget	High budget
Mixing Engineer	$500/day = $4,000	$1,500/day = $12,000	$2,500/day = $20,000
Mix Asst.	N/A	$400/day = $3,200	$1,000/day = $8,000
Studio	Home/private studio included in fee	$500/day = $4,000	$1,200/day = $9,600
Equipment Rental	N/A	N/A	$500/day = $4,000
Total	$4,000	$19,200	$41,600

Keep in mind that there are countless variants when pricing a mix, and these 3 budgets are for general reference. Engineer rates can vary, as can assistant rates and studio costs. I've seen top mixers do some projects at a discounted rate in their home studio with no assistant to help keep costs down, and I've seen them mix on a scoring stage or a large dub stage like at Technicolor Sound with top-notch assistants in which case overall costs can be even higher.

I've experienced mixers being flown to London to both record and mix a score, meaning there are travel costs involved that need to be added. I've also seen mixers manage as few as 5 minutes a day or as many as 20! You'll want to discuss your specific needs with your engineer to work out your actual schedule and cost. As you can see there are all sorts of variables that can affect your actual costs.

Mix Sessions

After the recording is done, all the live takes have been comped, at which point the sessions are ready to be sent to the mix. Following is a screenshots of the same session I included above in Part 6 Ptro Tools Prep, but this time with the live comped recordings. You'll notice I trimmed the beginning, end and extended periods of silence in the recorded tracks to ensure there are no accidental room noises in the final mix. Obviously, there are a lot more tracks now, so there are 4 pages to scroll through rather than just 2 as before. For this cue we recorded strings and choir. Notice the colors are consistent across the live and pre-record tracks. The pre-records are active and unmuted in case the mixer chooses to blend them with the live strings and choir, which is often the case.

Preparing for Scoring Sessions

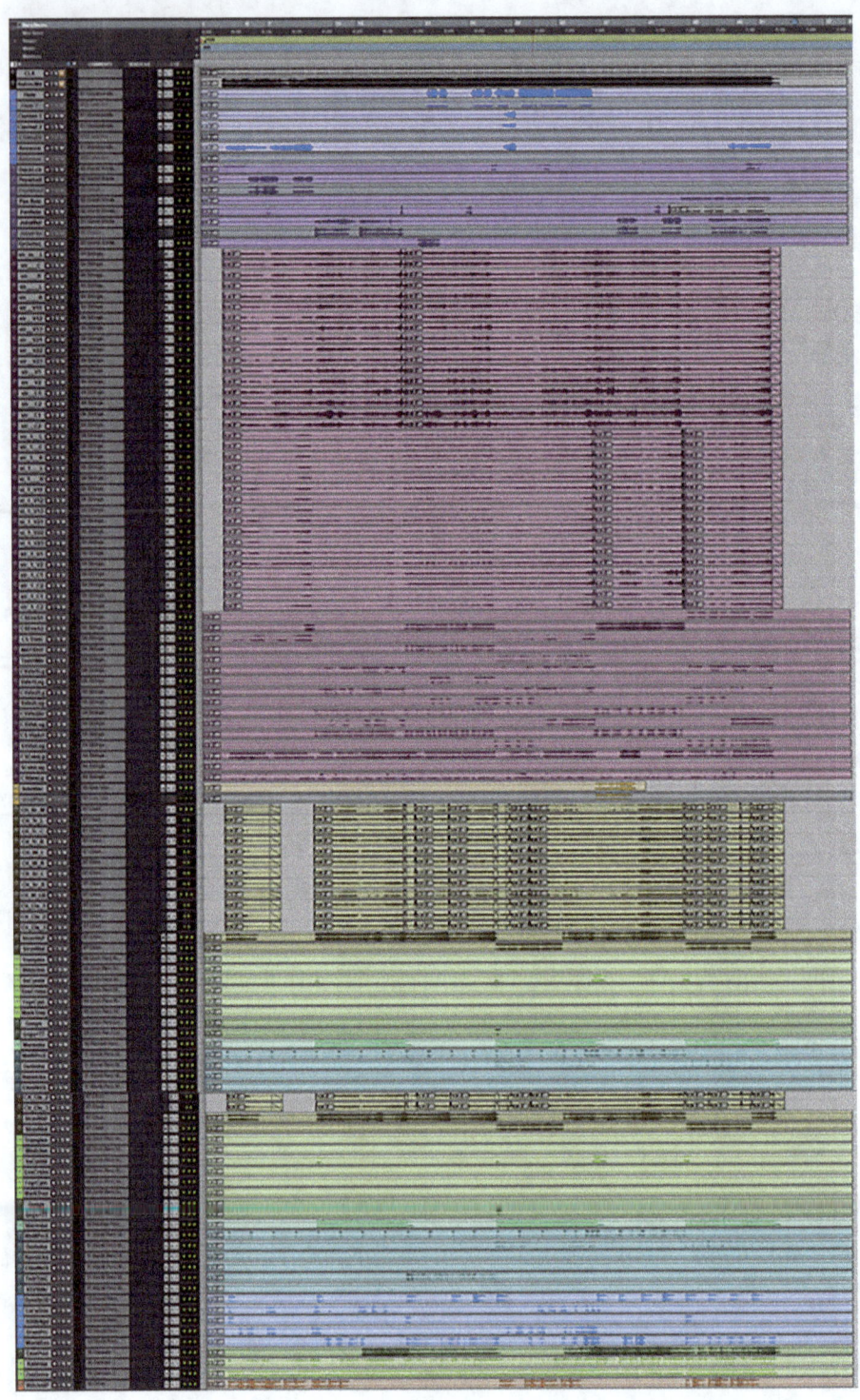

Layout Consistency

Once the mix is done and it's time to print, it's helpful to keep the exact same stem numbers and names along with the colors that were used in the mix sessions. Print all stems, even if that means creating an empty stem. When the stem count varies from one cue to the next it makes one question if anything is missing. When empty stems are printed and every cue has the exact same number of stems, it's crystal clear that nothing is missing. Make sure all stems are the exact same length. If there is need to re-print any stems, make sure the re-print is the exact same length as the original. If several stems are different lengths, it raises suspicion that there may be problems just as I described above when printing pre-records. As suggested earlier when printing pre-records, it's best to always print mixes staring at bar one.

Here is a screenshot of what delivery of final mix stems looks like for the above cue. As you can see the colors match the colors in the mix session. Some mixers don't send a session, but simply the audio files on their own. Either way works.

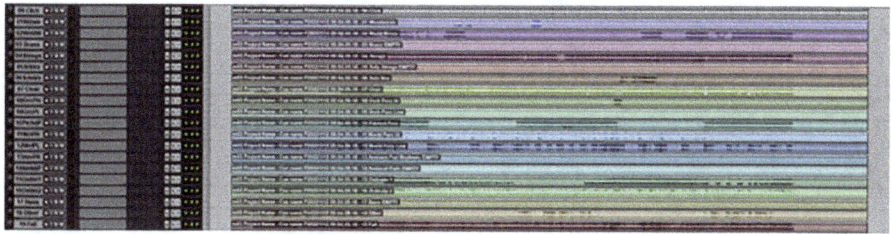

Stems File Naming

Earlier I said I think it's good practice to print empty stems to avoid questions of missing stems. However, when receiving a stem with no audio it could raise the question if this is intentional

Preparing for Scoring Sessions

or a misprint. Therefore, when printing an empty stem, add the word "EMPTY" or "BLANK" after the stem name. This is also another exception to my aversion to CAPS. This makes it crystal clear that the stem is supposed to be empty, eliminating questions or concerns. By clearly labeling it EMPTY or BLANK it's clear that it's not a misprint. For example:

"1m01 MAP Main Titles v3 P20221214 TC 1.03.14.12 - 12 Other EMPTY"

Addendum Two
Dub Session Prep

Once the mix is done and all the mix stems have been delivered, it's time to build the dub stage session and deliver the score. Building a dub stage session is pretty straight forward. Check with the dub stage if they want individual sessions for each reel, or a single super-session with all reels in it.

To start, create your session(s) and import the appropriate video and guide tracks.

Next, create tracks to match your stem layout. Many re-recording mixers like to have the music A/Bd or checkerboarded, meaning having 2 sets of tracks, in which case make a 2nd set of tracks and label the first set "A" and the second "B". Group your stems, if you have 2 sets create 2 groups, one for each. Import your cues and spot them to the timecode where they belong and that's pretty much all there is to it. If you're using 2 sets of tracks, the first

Preparing for Scoring Sessions

cue will go on the first set, the second cue on the second set, the third cue back on the first set of stems and so on.

If you have a lot of stems, especially if they are in large surround formats like 7.1 they'll use up lots of voices, and a single set of tracks might be better. Discuss this with your re-recoding mixer. If you use this method, make sure to create crossfades if cues overlap.

Once your audio files have been imported, you'll see the waveforms in the clips in your tracks. I like to trim the empty space at the beginning of each clip, so the music begins just a frame or two after the clips begin. This gives the re-recording mixer a more accurate visual of where the music really plays vs. having several seconds of silence at the beginning of the clips. I always add a short fade in (usually just a frame or two) to make sure there are no accidental pops or tics, and then add a fade out in the silence after the tail out of the music ends for the same reason. If there is an excessively long bit of silence at the end, I'll trim that, too. Finally, add a 2-pop and tail-pop. Some re-recording mixers want the pops on all tracks, others just want them on a single track, check with them before preparing your session and act accordingly. You can use the built-in signal generator plug in in the audio suite to create your pops, select a sine wave at -20dB.

That's it. You're ready to deliver your score. Whether I'm delivering a physical drive, or via dropbox or some other online delivery app I clear all unused clips from the session and save a copy of the session with all the audio. This ensures I have a single session folder with all the related audio in one place and I don't have to worry about the recipient having to link to audio in other folders. It's that copy that I send to the stage. If I have the video and audio guide tracks in the sessions, I'll create a separate "Video Deliverables" folder and put those there, and then manually delete them from each Session folder since saving a copy with all audio will make new copies of these files for each session, which is unnecessary.

Here are 3 examples of dub stage deliveries of a TV episode. The first screenshot is something I've seen people do and an example of what **not** to do.

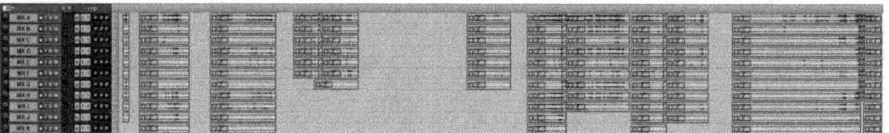

As you can see, there is no checker-boarding even though there aren't that many stems. The tracks are just labeled MX A-K giving no indication of what stem is on each track, and there is no consistency in the stem count or layout. The clips aren't trimmed, there are no fades and no 2 pop or tail pop. Can a re-recording mixer manage if this is what you deliver? Sure. But it's really not great.

Next is an example of the same thing, this time properly labeling the tracks and placing stems in the corresponding tracks consistently.

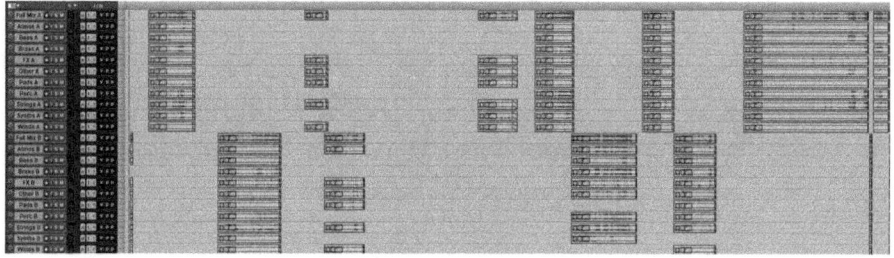

Preparing for Scoring Sessions

As you can tell, this is much better, but the missing clips raise a question. Is something missing? Or is there nothing there intentionally? Note there is checkerboarding, though we start with the bottom set of stems and in the middle of the session there are two cues on the same set of tracks rather than going back and forth. It's fine, but it's not great.

Finally, this is what I consider the proper way to deliver music to a dub stage.

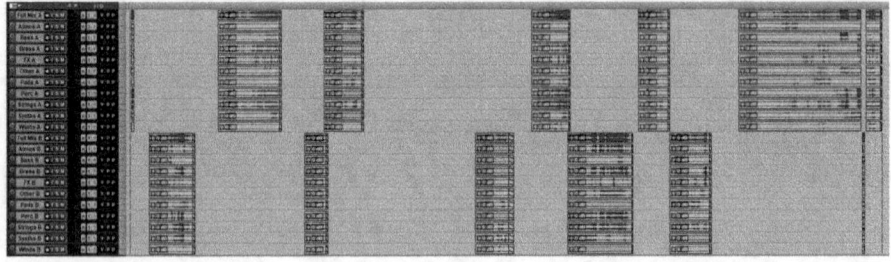

Notice the tracks are labeled indicating what's on them. I muted empty tracks, which gives the re-recording mixer a visual cue indicating there's nothing on those stems. The very first track is the stereo mix, which I muted so we're not doubling up on the full mix + the stems. It's there in case the re-recording mixer wants it for any reason, but the sum of the stems should equal the stereo mix and so playing the stems at the same level produces the same end result. I also muted any empty clips to give the mixer a visual cue so they don't have to wonder why nothing's coming out of that track.

This is a beautiful and well-built session for a dub stage. Any re-recording mixer who receives this will be very appreciative. This is a professional looking dub stage session.

Final Thoughts

I hope this booklet provides you with some clear and valuable insights, tips and ideas on every aspect of how to prepare for scoring sessions. As you can see, there are a lot of moving parts and lots of details to consider and account for, but the sum of all these details equals stress-free, smooth, and efficient sessions. To be honest, when I started writing this booklet, I thought I was writing a blog post that might span a few pages. I t wasn't until breaking everything down that I realized just how much is involved and it expanded to a full-blown booklet. After so many years of doing this, it really has become second nature for me. As you start to implement these suggestions and turn them into habits, I'm sure this will become easier and practically automatic as you gain experience over time.

The greatest reward of all this prep work is that moment

Preparing for Scoring Sessions

when brilliant musicians bring the music to life, and you can truly savor and enjoy it because everything is running smoothly. To me, even after all these years, it's still one of the greatest and most exhilarating experience there is.

About the Author

Composer and music editor Shie Rozow (pronounced shy ro-zov) has taken a different path than most leading him to work on over 150 feature films including major international blockbusters like *The Flash*, *The Lost City*, *Guardians of the Galaxy*, and *Hustle & Flow*.

Armed with over 25 years of industry experience and driven by his lifelong passion for music and storytelling, Shie has earned 17 Golden Reel Award Nominations, winning for his work on *Chicago* (as assistant music editor), *IMAX: Deep Sea*, and *Wu Tang: An American Saga*. He brings his inexhaustible talent and natural ear for music to every story, weaving a rich musical narrative that compliments the filmmaker's vision and unlocks new layers of depth.

Equally skilled working in film, TV, and video games, Shie has contributed his talent on hundreds of hours of TV including *Desperate Housewives*, *Arrow*, and most recently The CW's *Stargirl*, along with Amazon's anthology series *Welcome to the Blumhouse* and Shudder's *Creepshow*. In addition, he has also worked on music for Disney theme parks and Cirque du Soleil. Shie also composes concert music, which has been performed from coast to coast, releasing his first album *Musical Fantasy* in 2016.

You can hear his music on Netflix's documentary *Shawn Mendes: In Wonder* as well as award-winning indie features like *Jasmine, Camp Arrowhead, Captain Hagen's Bed and Breakfast,* and the feature documentary *The Last of the Winthrops.* His scores to *Matt and Maya, Lost Time, One Day You'll Go Blind,* and *Body Language: Bill Shannon* have all won Telly Awards.

A graduate of Berklee College of Music, where he completed his 4-year degree in just 5 semesters, ("being broke is a great incentive," he explained), Shie lives in Los Angeles with his wife, two children, and their many pets. He enjoys photography, astronomy and SCUBA diving in his free time.

To learn more about Shie and his work, visit his website at www.shierozow.com.

www.ingramcontent.com/pod-product-compliance
Lightning Source LLC
Chambersburg PA
CBHW070435010526
44118CB00014B/2046